Praise for From Doubl

Tyrelle Smith has created a roadmap for believers into discovering what it means to truly walk in faith and integrity. She explains how the Holy Spirit helped her discern areas where her mind had been divided, and how He brought her to a place of victory and spiritual wholeness. She delivers the keys to having a single, sound mind with a heart that is fully devoted to the Lord and established in truth and faith. This wonderful book will be a great blessing to your walk with Jesus.
--**Daniel Kolenda**, President and CEO, *Christ for all Nations*

If you're longing to feel connected with a writer who understands your doubts and has walked through many of the trials you are facing in regards to your destiny, this book is for you. Tyrelle will take you on a personal journey of understanding God's heart for your life and how He desires to help you live out your calling. Her passion to share with you, her precious reader, about the crucial importance of living a single-minded life to fulfill your mandate from God is evident in every page. From relatable stories to Biblical truths, Tyrelle's book will captivate your attention as you long to know more of how you can righteously fulfill God's plan and purpose for your life.
--**Jeri Hill**, President, *Together In The Harvest*

Tyrelle Smith is a voice crying in the wilderness, calling the church back to the purity of the Gospel. Tyrelle shares out of her own life experience of being double-minded to forsaking all to follow Christ. She has deep Biblical insights and practical applications. I highly recommend this book.
--**Harvey Katz**, Author, *Becoming A God Magnet*

Tyrelle Smith is an amazing woman of God who has triumphed in the area of her identity and destiny in Christ. Her book *From Double Minded to Destiny* is

both insightful and liberating. If you apply what is written in these pages with the guidance of the Holy Spirit, this book will change your life.
--Matthew Russell, Lead Evangelist, *World for Christ*

In *From Double-minded to Destiny*, Tyrelle Smith has a refreshing look at dealing with a double-minded heart. Weaving in personal stories with explanations in scripture, she has a fresh and energizing perspective in dealing with personal struggles.

The reflective questions at the end of each chapter are thought-provoking, providing the reader with a mirror to determine their personal status and illuminate the necessary steps to a healthy single-minded heart. *From Double Minded to Destiny* is a wonderful tool for developing the devoted undistracted heart required to enter destiny.
--Richard and Joanne Lepp, Founders of *Joseph Group Incorporated*, and personal mentors to Bill and Tyrelle Smith

Double-mindedness is a problem we all face. We can probably trace its roots back to specific experiences in our lives. As I journaled through this book, the Lord reminded me of the key event which brought double-mindedness into my life, and told me to set it aside as I did not have full understanding concerning it. I have chosen to do that and to speak in faith those things the Lord tells me to speak, knowing that in doing so, I am speaking them into existence. The Bible says that what I say "shall" happen (Mk. 11:23). So we need to speak only words of life. This book will help you do that as it helped me. According to your faith is a refrain from Scripture, and a double-minded person receives nothing from the Lord. How precious is a book which walks us out of wavering unbelief? Priceless, I would say. Thank you, Tyrelle, for this gift to our lives.
--**Dr Mark Virkler**, President, *Communion with God Ministries*

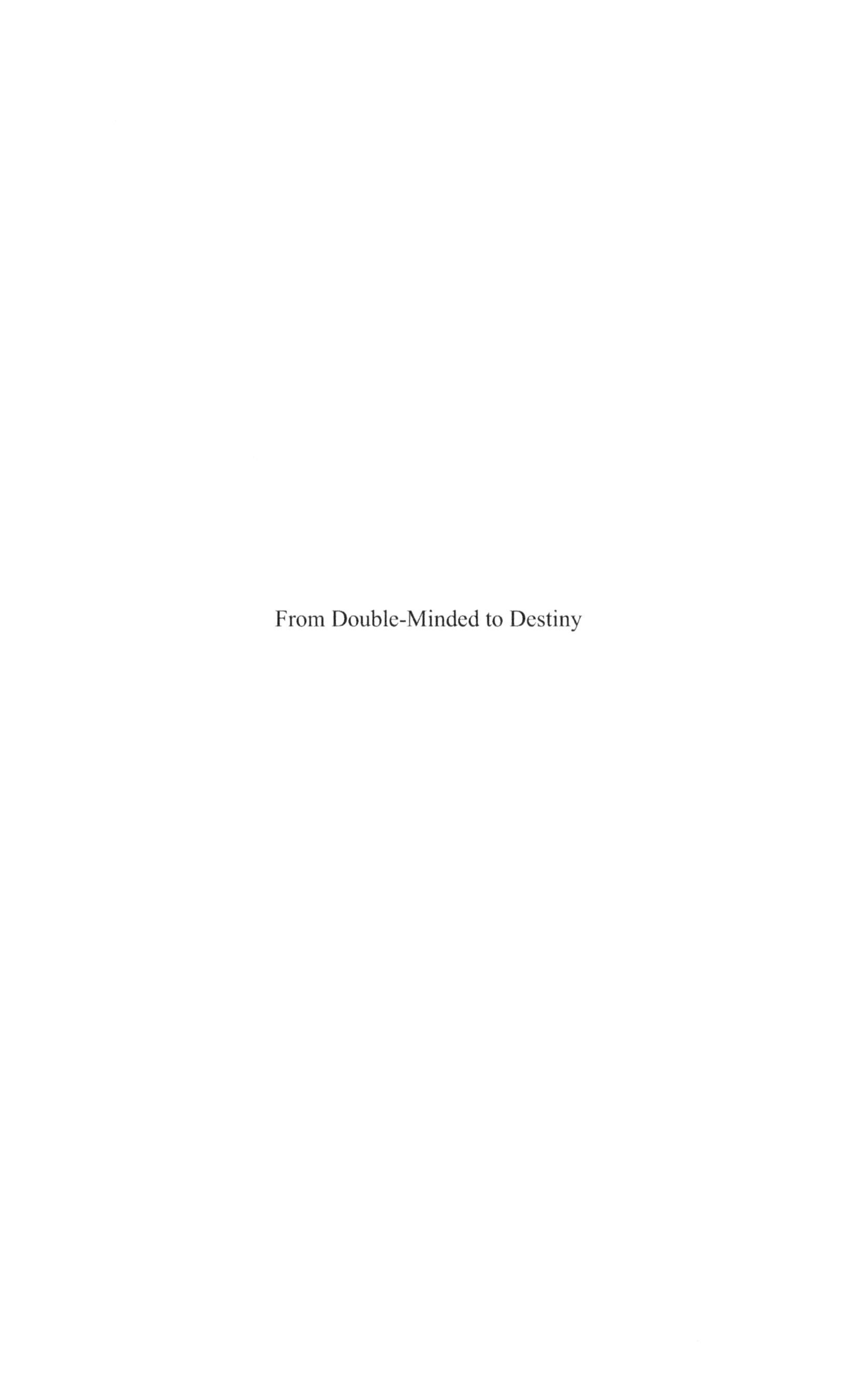

From Double-Minded to Destiny

From Double-Minded

To Destiny

How to stand firm in your faith with an undivided heart and singleness of mind.

Tyrelle Smith

Gospel Fire Publishing
Canada
2019

ISBN: 978-1-9992251-0-0 (Paperback)
ISBN: 978-1-9992251-1-7 (eBook)
ISBN: 978-1-9992251-2-4 (Audio Book)

Cover Photo: Brittney-June Photography
Cover Design: Bill Smith
Interior Design: Bill Smith

DEDICATION

I dedicate this book to the five most influential men in my life. First to my wonderful husband, Bill Smith, who has shown me the love, forgiveness, honor, and strength of my Beloved Jesus Christ. And second, to my Dad, Ernest Paterson, who has shown me what My Father in Heaven was like, long before I ever met Him. I see my God in you both and I worship Him. May the Lord bless you. For when You grant a blessing, O Lord, it is an eternal blessing!

— 1 Chronicles 17:26–27, NLT

And to my three powerful and wonderful sons, William, Ezekiel, and Samuel, I love you and thank you for enriching my life. You are my greatest accomplishments. I have no greater joy than seeing you walk in truth. Thank you for choosing truth. I love the men you have become. You exemplify this masculine verse: Be watchful, stand firm in the faith, act like men, be strong. Let all that you do be done in love.

— 1 Corinthians 16:13-14, ESV

And also, Gillianne Cheryl Paterson, my mom and forever friend. You are wisdom in my night parables by which I learn from the King. You are cautionary love to the Body of Christ as I sleep, that I might speak correction, insight and encouragement to the body when I wake. God uses mothers to train the world.

— Proverbs 1:8-9, ESV

TABLE OF CONTENTS

FOREWORD

You can instantly tell a lot about a person when you're sitting across from them in snowy Saskatchewan, Canada enjoying a hot cappuccino and conversations of spiritual-depth. I don't know about you, but if you've picked up this book, you're probably desiring to go deeper in your intimate relationship with God. You and Tyrelle already have something in common, then.

From the moment I met my precious friend, I immediately knew without a doubt that she had a hunger for God and a burden for people. Tyrelle's heart is humble and her character has been refined and tested through God's Word. In this book, she has a beautiful desire, to see you thrive in your walk with God.

Tyrelle is just like you and me, she is driven and determined to fulfill God's purpose for her life. But just like so many of us, we've heard numerous times about "fulfilling your purpose," yet oftentimes we are left longing to know what that actually looks like. What does it look like to follow Jesus Christ and live out this so-called destiny He has for us? And how do we effectively attain it?

From the moment you read the first page in *From Double-Minded To Destiny*, you instantly understand Tyrelle's love for the reader - for you. My heart was grasped as I read her opening story of God revealing to her how deeply crucial it is to follow the words in Scripture. From the beginning word to the very last page, she explains in each compelling chapter that we cannot simply read the Bible, but we must first have a revelation of the words on the pages; then the more daring part, we need to actually live them out.

Maybe you have felt lost or confused in believing God about what your purpose truly is. In order to achieve anything in life, there will be obstacles and uncertainties, but through the pages in this book, we learn how to understand the heart of God for us and how He sees us. It doesn't matter what man thinks or what culture is doing around us, what matters is that we are living according to God's truth of being single-minded which is found in His Word.

If you're searching for answers as to why you've felt defeated or halted in your journey of life with God. If you're wondering why you've questioned so much or felt resistance in trusting the Lord. If you've felt frustrated, confused and lost in walking out your calling, I believe wholeheartedly your spirit will feel revived and ready to accomplish your God-given purpose here on earth after reading this book.

However, in order to effectively accomplish your mission, you must first strip away all of the mindsets and thoughts that don't align with God's Word. Through educating ourselves about stability all throughout the Bible and relying on the Holy Spirit for guidance, we can be assured that God will help direct us on the narrow path of righteousness as we walk out our mandate from Him.

As you begin to turn these pages, get ready for a phenomenal journey. I challenge you to allow the Holy Spirit to give you revelation as you read each page. Ask Him to breathe new life and excitement into your heart. Believe that He will give you clarity, direction and peace as you seek His voice in the truth of Tyrelle's words and scriptures. Allow her personal experiences to become the shoulders upon which you stand. Now is the time to live out a life that is undivided for Christ! I believe *From Double-Minded To Destiny* will encourage you to be commissioned in truth for Him!

Let the journey begin…

Jeri Hill
President, *Together In The Harvest*
Orlando, FL
Togetherintheharvest.com

INTRODUCTION

Standing firm and steadfast in your faith is one of the most important aspects of a believer's life. It's hard to be full of peace and joy when you are happy one minute and devastated, confused, or unable to stick with decisions the next. But your life can be full of peace and joy! God wants this for you, but it requires relentless trust in Him.

Trust can be easier said than done, especially if you are prone to worry, fear, or have past hurts or trauma. Sometimes there are things people desire that can hinder their ability to trust and believe; without realizing it, they are out of alignment with God. But God wants *you* to know that He is good and is willing to bring you to a place where you are calm, steady, and powerful as you walk with Him. Whatever your situation, you can be sure that your victory, peace, and stability are God's priority.

The fact that you picked up this book reflects an internal cry to the Father that though you are struggling and hurting, you desire to live strong and anchored in His secure love. Many people today are struggling, tossed to and fro in their thoughts, and desperate for peace—but not finding it. They want to trust God but don't know *how* to trust Him. Not only has God provided the necessary answers in His Word, He desires to partner with you to help you stand firm *as you trust in Him.*

...Because God is good, you can trust that His ways and words are also good and will not fail you. Clinging to and building upon God's Word will lead to a solid foundation. Isaiah 54:14 says, "In righteousness you will be established" (NIV). So, no matter what storms come, when you are anchored in God's Word, you will not be like a house that falls or a storm-tossed wave on the ocean of life's circumstances. You will be solid.

Stability comes from trusting God and who He is—His love will never fail. Just as good parents want their kids to be confident, full of peace, and ready to take on the world, God wants His children to know He is with them, supports them, and that they can count on Him. He created you with amazing plans in mind. As you trust the love and character of God, you will be steady and strong, able to fulfill His assignments for your life.

But becoming steady and peaceful in God will take some time. I'm not talking about taking the time to do your morning devotions, although that is a good place to start. I am talking about taking a season with the Lord to sort through the things causing the challenges you're facing and re-ordering them, together with Him. He will reveal areas that make you storm-tossed and afflicted and will then establish a firm foundation in your life (Isa. 54:11). He delights in turning His children's weaknesses into strengths. *I know because He did it for me.*

The first half of the book will help you purify your heart, so you can get free of doubt and instability. The second half of the book will help you put your new wholeheartedness into believing God's unfailing love and character and learning to stand firm in your faith, win life's battles and fulfill your God given assignments - your destiny.

This book is the culmination of a year of learning who the Lord is and what His love is really like. It was a year of learning about and experiencing His faithfulness to me—and learning about how He is faithful to every person He has created. The beauty of God is that His love never ends and never runs out; therefore, neither do His glorious lessons. I invite you to join me, together with the Lord, on this journey to becoming like a nail in a sure place . . . steadfast, immovable, and always abounding in the work of the Lord (1 Cor. 15:58).

A Prophetic Cry of Anguish

"How long... How long… How long will you waver between two opinions?" I heard Him cry. It resonated in my chest and reverberated through the spirit realm; a cry of anguish. It was the cry of God for His people; the voice of the Father crying out in anguish over his dear children. He continued, "I can't bear it any longer. If I am the Lord, serve Me. If your lovers - your idols - are God, serve them. Why waver between two opinions?"

Day after day, I heard Him cry in anguish, "How long will you waver? How long…"

As I waited on the Lord, I asked Him to speak to me in my sleep. That night, I dreamed nothing at all… but I heard His audible voice saying, "Blessed are the pure in heart…"

My soul answered the rest of the verse like an old song I knew by heart - the promise "… for they shall see God," Then I awoke and went downstairs to wait on Him. I sat in my chair, and as His Presence fell, so did my tears.

It is a clarion call to the whole body. It's His voice crying out in the wilderness. If we do not harden our hearts, we will enter the promise, "we shall see God!" His words echoed and ricocheted in my soul, "Blessed are the pure in heart, blessed are the pure in heart, blessed are the pure in heart." It was a call to purity. It was an invitation. It was a command. And it was a promise.

As I continued to wait in His presence, He brought to mind an early encounter He had with Peter. Jesus spoke from Peter's boat to the multitudes, Peter heard Jesus preach the Word. It was a light shining into all the dark and hidden places of Peter's heart.

Jesus' light was shining but Peter was hiding; retreating into the darkness, saying, "Depart from me for I am a sinful man." Although Peter was looking at Jesus, what he was really seeing was himself. He was backing away, *but Jesus was leaning in.* He pursued Peter and said, "Follow Me." You can hear Him calling... "Follow! Be one who builds your life on what you see Me do and what you hear Me say. Leave those things that keep you from Me. Don't retreat ...follow! Come into this light, this righteousness, and do all that you see Me do." Then Jesus gave the promise, "... and I will make you a fisher of men."

Peter did not harden his heart. He did not look at the multitude of fish on the sand that he could sell. He did not look at his family situation or the previous sinful pleasures in his life. He looked at Jesus alone. He dropped his nets and followed, and so he entered into the promise and his purpose.

A week later, I was sitting with my husband outside on the patio drinking coffee. He was smiling at me the way husbands smile at their wives, and I was struck suddenly in my heart: How can he look at me like that after twenty-three years? I have wrinkles, and things are sagging in places that used to be firm and tight. I marveled for a moment. Then I started to cry because of his love for me and his devotion. He chose me, and he has not let his eyes wander, or his heart.

I walked over to him, bent down and kissed his head and thanked him. Jesus spoke clearly to my heart and said, "I wish My church, My people looked at Me the way he looks at you... that her heart would not wander... that her eyes would not wander but out of utter devotion, loyalty and love, she would look only at Me."

Eyes don't wander on their own. The eyes wander because the heart wanders when it's tempted and lured away by another desire. That heart belongs partly to a wife and partly to another desire... it is a mixture, not purely one thing or the other. But the pure in heart see God.

God has betrothed us to His Son and the bride price was His blood and death on the cross. The Holy Spirit cried out through Paul the apostle for our pure and simple devotion to that Son, Jesus:

> For I am jealous for you with a godly jealousy; for I betrothed you to one husband, so that to Christ I might present you as a pure virgin. But I am afraid that, as the serpent deceived Eve by his craftiness, your minds will be led astray from pure and simple devotion to Christ.
>
> -2 Corinthians 11:2-3 NASB

There is a voice crying out as it did in Elijah's day, "How long will you waver between two opinions? If the Lord is God serve Him. If Baal is God serve Him." (1 Kings 18:21) The nation did not fully serve God or Baal. Their heart was divided between their false loves and God, tossing them back and forth.

But God was looking at them through the eyes of Elijah saying, "Follow Me."

Today, Jesus is speaking! His word is pure and is a purifier. His voice is righteousness and it's light and we can retreat from it or we can enter into this moment. Don't look away. Look Jesus in the eyes. He's inviting, He's commanding and He's consecrating unto a purpose. Don't waver. Follow, and inherit. He's promising, saying, "Blessed, blessed, blessed are the pure in heart …" and let our response be, "...for we will see God."

As we see Him, gazing with eyes wide open, we follow Him into our purpose and our destiny; Jesus receiving the reward of His suffering through our passionate, obedient, faith-filled lives.

PART I - REMOVING THE SECOND HEAD

Do the words storm-tossed and afflicted describe you? Do you feel your life represents a wave tossed to and fro driven by the various winds described in James 1:7? Do you identify with the words "double-minded and unstable in all his ways?" Do you struggle with confusion or making up your own mind without polling people around you? Are you not able to make clear decisions or follow through with decisions you do make? Do you struggle with thoughts that end up exhausting you? Or obsessive negative thinking? The good news is that you are not alone. These are symptoms of double-mindedness and becoming single-minded is God's great plan for you. God is with you and He wants to lead you to victory. In the first half of the book, we will journey together to root out the sources of double-mindedness, so you can be rooted in God's love and faithfulness, stand firm without wavering, and live out your destiny for His glory.

Take your time with the Holy Spirit in each chapter of the book. Journal this journey as you process together towards your destiny. You are right where He wants you to be; here and in the palm of His hands and you are going to win!

If you want to learn more about listening to the Holy Spirit, see Appendix A, How to Hear God's Voice, by Dr. Mark Virkler, for beautiful and simple instructions on incorporating journaling into your journey From Double-Minded to Destiny.

Chapter 1 – The Only True Stability

I will make him like a nail in a sure place. — Isaiah 22:23

Two Heads? Cutting off the Second Head!

During one season, I was experiencing an intense crisis in believing God and that His promises and leadings would come to pass in my life. I was afraid to step into my calling due to the fear of man. Finally, one day it came to a head. I was in the dumps, miserable, unbelieving, and untrusting—and there is no joy or peace when choosing not to trust God, I'll tell you that! On this day, the battle was thick.

I probably should have sought God more personally, but instead, I took the easy way out and called my aunt. She and Jesus are very close; she submits her whole life to Him. Well, God knew I would fail in my faith, and "The Great Set Up" was about to begin. She answered after a few rings, but before I could say a word, my aunt relayed an intense dream she had the night before. In her dream, she had two heads. Looking in a mirror, she had to take a sword and cut off one of the heads. My aunt is sweet and kind and cutting anything but chicken for dinner is horrific for her! This was a prophetic picture of double-mindedness and was a modern-day parable, sent by God, to set me free.

James wrote that those who doubt are like "a wave of the sea driven and tossed by the wind," and they are "double-minded" and "unstable." The word "double-minded" comes from the Greek word *dipsuchos* (Strong's G1364, G5590) and means, "to be two-souled or two-headed and two-minded, wavering, uncertain, or having a divided interest/loyalty." God, however, desires His children be single-minded, unwavering, devoted to and loving Him with "all their heart, soul, mind, and strength." God uses Isaiah the prophet to illustrate what stability and single-mindedness looks like saying, "I will make him like a nail in a sure place" (Is. 22:23). A nail in a sure place does not waver but remains both fixed and firm.

The Bible teaches that out of the abundance of a person's heart, the mouth speaks (Luke 6:45). When your heart is divided between two loyalties, it is like having two heads and thus two mouths speaking two arguing viewpoints. This was the state I found myself in that day. Imagine having two heads, one speaking the mind of Christ and the other nattering the mind of the enemy. To remain in a place of peace, there cannot be two nattering heads talking at the same time.

One head speaks truth loyally for God, saying that with God all things are possible. He can be trusted, and He will do what He says. This head whispers for us to simply trust and obey God. The other head springs from a loyalty to the world rooted in selfish desires that has an antichrist spirit in nature; this head does not believe the things of God. It woos us to question God's Word and draws us away from Jesus and into our own desires. Jesus warned against a split in devotion, saying, "No one can serve two masters. Either he will hate the one and love the other, or he will be devoted to the one and despise the other" (Matt. 6:24). Jesus' nature is giving, but the love of the world is selfish; because of this, they will always be at war within the person who is devoted to both. It's like soldiers fighting in a war but are loyal to both sides; victory on the battlefield is impossible.

James vividly describes the double-minded person using imagery of a surging wave, tossed back and forth by the wind. The person whose loyalty is divided both affirms and denies God's truth. The New Bible Commentary calls this inner cleavage to two loyalties "doubt." Those who doubt rise to the heavens to receive the promise—but they plunge to the depths, equally sure it will not be fulfilled. James taught that followers of Jesus should not be double-minded, believing God one minute and doubting Him the next and explained how double-mindedness creates instability in a person's life. He paints for us a strong word picture of this internal battle of divided loyalty:

> If any of you lacks wisdom, let him ask of God, who gives to all liberally and without reproach, and it will be given to him. But let him ask in faith, with no doubting, for he who doubts is like a wave of the sea driven and tossed by the wind. For let not that man suppose that he will receive anything from the Lord; he is a double-minded man, unstable in all his ways.
>
> — James 1:5-8, NKJV

James explains to us that the root of double-mindedness is in the purity of the heart and that it is up to us to purify it:

> Therefore, submit to God. Resist the devil and he will flee from you. Draw near to God and He will draw near to you. Cleanse your hands, you sinners; and purify your hearts, you double-minded.
>
> — James 4:7-8, NKJV

James declared that if believers resist Satan, he must leave. The best model for resisting the devil is Jesus. When Satan tempted Jesus in the wilderness with the lust of the flesh by offering Him bread, Jesus fought the battle with the Word of God. He put His Father's will and His people's needs above His own desire to eat the bread using the Word of God to cut off the second head, with its loyalties and temptations. The writer of Hebrews affirmed the power of the Word of God to fight the enemy:

> For the word of God is living and active, sharper than any two-edged sword, piercing to the division of soul and of spirit, of joints and of marrow, and discerning the thoughts and intentions of the heart.
>
> — Hebrews 4:12, NASB

Truth comes when a person is desperate and acknowledges their need for it—and God hears his or her cry. He loves to release His truth to set people free into the abundant life He died to give them.

After my phone call with my aunt, I was at the end of myself; I had tried everything I knew. As I stood before God, I cried out from a point of deep weakness: "God, make me a nail in a sure place. Turn my weakness into strength. If you don't show me what is wrong, I can't change. Help me, God. Show me why I am struggling!"

I knew the Lord who sees all things had my answer, so I continued my plea: "Lord, I want to be stable and firm, immovable, and at peace. Help me, God. I need a word!" I knew His truth would set me free, and I welcomed it. Even if it pierced my heart, I knew His truth would also bring healing and restoration. Tears filled my eyes. I was embarrassed and ashamed of my weaknesses and I told Him so. I also knew the One who formed me and loved me heard my cry.

I was ready to end my struggle with double-mindedness. My soul was storm-tossed and afflicted. Confusion and doubt often plagued me; I would poll people before making decisions, and when I finally made one, I struggled to follow through with what I had decided. My thoughts exhausted me as they pulled me back and forth.

My mind trailed to the words from an online devotional I had read that day, and I saw it—the word from the Lord that would start the ball rolling toward my God-given freedom. This word from Isaiah would be the beginning of a teaching for all who would need it:

> I publicly proclaim bold promises. I do not whisper obscurities in some dark corner. I would not have told the people of Israel to seek me if I could not be found. I, the Lord, speak only what is true and declare only what is right.
>
> — Isaiah 45:19, NLT

Isaiah painted a picture of where true steadfastness and singleness of mind may be found in God alone. God is not double-minded or unsure; He only speaks what He fully sees, with undivided commitment. No man can do that … only God. What character!

The Revelation

Suddenly, I understood. Double-mindedness had kept me from the ability to believe God and place my trust completely in Him. That explained why I was not moving forward in my God-given destiny. It's those who know and believe their God that do great exploits. God wants to deal with our divided loyalties so we can believe in His faithfulness, love and goodness and accomplish our God-given destinies. Our destinies change the world.

Satan has been crafty in dividing our loyalties. He has made many of us doubters, but Jesus will make us believers as we purify our hearts.

A Single-Minded God

To bear witness to the truth, one must act on the conviction of it. The Father, Son, and Holy Spirit *are* truth, and are faithful to do what they say. That is why God can publicly proclaim a bold promise. Because He is all knowing—seeing the beginning and the end—He makes up His mind and follows His promises through to completion. He is committed and single-minded.

Look at this shining example from Numbers which affirms God's steadfast and faithful character:

> God is not a man, that He should lie, Nor a son of man, that He should change His mind;
> Has He said, and will He not do it? Or has He spoken, and will He not make it good?
>
> — Numbers 23:19, NLT

There is stability in God's faithfulness; He never lies or changes His mind. He longs to see us, His children, live and operate with this same stability. Although God made man in His image (Gen. 1:27), our character develops and becomes more like Him as we ponder and behold Him. God, however, doesn't develop; His character never changes. The Father doesn't just *have* love for His people—He *is* love (1 John 4:8). As a good Father, God instructs His children with wisdom that they might excel. Like any good father, God rejoices when

His children "get it right." Paul described God's divine joy rooted in love, which rejoices in truth, as evidenced when His people allow truth to win out in their lives rather than choosing unrighteousness (1 Cor. 13:6).

God sent the Holy Spirit to lead and guide us into all truth. He desires to help you root out anything that pulls your devotion back and forth like a storm-tossed wave, causing your heart to be divided. If you allow Him to work, your life will instead represent a nail in a sure place—it will be steadfast and immovable (Isa. 22:23). He has included everything a person needs in the Bible—including powerful examples of real people who followed Him and His ways—but who struggled as well. One such man was Jehoshaphat.

Jehoshaphat: A Real-Life Example of Stability

Jehoshaphat, one of Judah's kings, was an incredible man of God whose story can be found in 2 Chronicles 14–20. His life exemplified a faith and loyalty to God that blessed his own life and his nation. He was not perfect, but his heart was devoted to the Lord. God's Word was the foundation of his life. Jehoshaphat was King Asa's son, who also sought God:

> Asa did what was pleasing and good in the sight of the Lord his God. He removed the foreign altars and the pagan shrines. He smashed the sacred pillars and cut down the Asherah poles. He commanded the people of Judah to seek the Lord, the God of their ancestors, and to obey His law and commands.
>
> — 2 Chronicles 14:2–4, NLT

During King Asa's reign, the Ethiopians attacked Judah. King Asa won a great victory in battle by calling on the Lord. God, in His faithfulness, took Asa's armies as His own and soundly beat Judah's enemy. Through a prophet, God exhorted King Asa to be strong and courageous and establish his kingdom by teaching God's laws. Asa was to call God's people to implement God's laws individually in their lives; doing so would keep them from idolatry. Asa responded by ridding the land of false worship. Most importantly, he called his people to make a covenant with God—to seek Him with their entire heart and soul. The people shouted their oath of loyalty to the Lord with trumpet blasts. The chronicler wrote of this moment:

> All in Judah were happy about this covenant for they had entered into it with *all* their heart. They earnestly sought after God, and they found him. And the Lord gave them rest from their enemies on every side.
>
> — 1 Chronicles 15:12, 14–15, NLT

Imagine being Asa's child. He had witnessed his father's victory in battle, a clear result from his trust in God. What an impression this must have made upon young Jehoshaphat! Sadly, Jehoshaphat's father deteriorated spiritually and physically. He eventually died of a foot disease, leaving Jehoshaphat in charge of the kingdom.

But 2 Chronicles 17:3 says the Lord was with Jehoshaphat because he followed his father's earlier example. Jehoshaphat didn't worship false gods. He tore down pagan altars, sought his father's God, and obeyed God's commands. Because of this, Scripture says, "The Lord *established* Jehoshaphat's control over the kingdom of Judah" (2 Chron. 17:5). The word "establish" in the original Hebrew is interesting. It's the word *kuwn* (*Strong's* H3559), which means, "to be fixed, firm, faithfulness, fasten, ordain, perfect and order." It also means, "appoint, render sure, proper, or prosperous."[1] When God ordains, fixes, fastens, perfects, appoints, and renders a person sure, no one can undo what God has done. God "rendered sure" Jehoshaphat's control over Judah and no man could undo it.

Jehoshaphat not only tore down pagan altars, but he also encouraged a right belief system. He sent his most trusted officials—the Levites—to instruct Judah about God's ways and to inspire new and devoted hearts within God's beloved people.

---

[1]Strong, James. *The New Strong's Expanded Exhaustive Concordance of the Bible.* Nashville: Thomas Nelson Publishers 2010

Jehoshaphat's Battle with Double-Mindedness

Shortly after this, Jehoshaphat made an alliance with Ahab, a powerful king and an enemy of God who worshipped idols. Ahab could not have hit God harder than by robbing Him of His children's affection and faith. In the heat of battle, Jehoshaphat called on the Lord, and the Lord saved his life (2 Chron. 18:31). Nonetheless, God disciplined Jehoshaphat in love, sending Jehu, a prophet, to bring both a corrective word and encouragement to the king:

> When King Jehoshaphat of Judah arrived safely home in Jerusalem, Jehu son of Hanani the seer went out to meet him. "Why should you help the wicked and love those who hate the Lord?" he asked the king. "Because of what you have done, the Lord is very angry with you. Even so, there is some good in you, for you have removed the Asherah poles throughout the land, and you have committed yourself to seeking God."
>
> — 2 Chronicles 19:1–3, NLT

The Lord saw Jehoshaphat's sin, but also remembered the good Jehoshaphat had done in removing idol worship from the land. A part of Jehoshaphat was loyal to man, seen in his strategic alliance with Ahab. However, Jehoshaphat also trusted God who had established his kingdom. Jehoshaphat's loyalty was divided; he was double-minded. *And God was not unaware.*

Double-mindedness toward God may be likened to two best friends in school, Johnny and Steve. Each is the other's favorite. They pick each other first for everything. When the teacher says, "Get a partner," Johnny and Steve give each other "the look." You know the one; the "let's be partners" look. But Johnny also has an enemy in the class, Craig, who's super popular and has turned most of the class against him. Those who are friends with Craig are not only safe but also kind of cool.

One day, Johnny is late to school. During his absence, the teacher says, "Okay everyone, get a partner." Craig turns to Johnny's best friend Steve, gives him "the look," and even though he's uncomfortable, Steve concedes. Steve becomes Craig's partner. Not long after, Johnny arrives. Johnny sees Steve with his worst enemy. His face shows hurt, anger, and betrayal. Johnny sits down beside Steve and whispers angrily "I can't believe you did that. *Anybody* but Craig. Craig hates me and has even turned everyone away from me, too. *Why did you do that*?"

Jehoshaphat betrayed God, like Steve betrayed Johnny, by making an alliance with God's enemy. And yet, God's mercy to Jehoshaphat was incredible. He saw Jehoshaphat's mistake, but also the good Jehoshaphat had done. Your Father sees the good you have done as well.

Jehoshaphat sought to reverse his poor choices and strengthen his kingdom once again by teaching God's ways and commands. This created a space for the Word of God to fill the hearts of His people:

> These were [Jehoshaphat's] instructions to them: "You must always act in the fear of the LORD, with faithfulness *and an undivided heart*."
>
> — 2 Chronicles 19:9, NLT, emphasis added

Jehoshaphat had experienced the consequences of a divided heart and warned God's people against doing the same.

Jehoshaphat Stands Firm and Single-minded.

Despite seasons of doubt and double-mindedness, the best was yet to come for Jehoshaphat. His righteous government and religious systems were in place, and his relationship with God was on track. Then, one fateful day, three foreign armies attacked Judah. Jehoshaphat was alarmed, but He knew God's Word—and this time, he stood unwaveringly. He gathered the people to fast, pray, and seek the Lord according to 2 Chronicles 6:

> When Your people go out to battle against their enemies, wherever You send them, and when they pray to You toward this city which You have chosen and the temple which I have built for Your name,

> then hear from heaven their prayer and their supplication, and maintain their cause.
>
> — 2 Chronicles 6:34–35, NLT

From that place of obedience to God's *written* instructions, Jehoshaphat stood before the community of Judah and Jerusalem in front of the new courtyard at the temple of the Lord. He prayed and decreed to God who God was and why he and God's people were there:

> O Lord, God of our ancestors, you alone are the God who is in heaven. You are ruler of all the kingdoms of the earth. You are powerful and mighty; no one can stand against you! O our God, did you not drive out those who lived in this land when your people Israel arrived? And did you not give this land forever to the descendants of your friend Abraham? Your people settled here and built this Temple to honor your name. They said, "Whenever we are faced with any calamity such as war, plague, or famine, we can come to stand in your presence before this Temple where your name is honored. We can cry out to you to save us, and you will hear us and rescue us."
>
> — 2 Chronicles 20:6–9, NLT

In a time of uncertainty when war with surrounding nations was imminent, Jehoshaphat unwaveringly trusted God for guidance. This is what it means to have an undivided heart, to stand firm and be "a nail in a sure place."

Jehoshaphat had seen God's faithfulness in the past and knew He could be trusted. Jehoshaphat declared God's Word to Him in the presence of God's people and let God honor His own words and character by His actions. Then, he made his petition for rescue. Despite all the warriors and wealth that Jehoshaphat possessed, he trusted the Lord alone for victory. He sought the power and throne of God before the power and thrones of men. Not knowing his next steps, Jehoshaphat then cried out to God:

> We don't know what to do, but we are looking to you for help.
>
> — 2 Chronicles 20:12, NLT

As the men of Judah stood before the Lord with their families, the Spirit of the Lord came upon a man named Jahaziel who declared:

> Listen, all you people of Judah and Jerusalem! Listen, King Jehoshaphat! This is what the Lord says: Do not be afraid! Don't be discouraged by this mighty army, for the battle is not yours, but God's. Tomorrow, march out against them. You will find them coming up through the ascent of Ziz at the end of the valley that opens into the wilderness of Jeruel. But you will not even need to fight. Take your positions; then stand still and watch the Lord's victory. He is with you, O people of Judah and Jerusalem. Do not be afraid or discouraged. Go out against them tomorrow, for the Lord is with you!
>
> — 2 Chronicles 20:13–17, NLT

God responded to Jehoshaphat's obedience by giving assurance of the victory. Twice in this passage, God told Jehoshaphat and the people not to be afraid or discouraged, and twice He reminded them the victory was His. The Lord, more committed in love than mere people, because He *is* love, promised that His presence would not leave them. He reminded His people that though no foreign king was fighting alongside them, nor any sidekick armies, God Himself was executing His own battle plan; He would fight on behalf of a people whose hearts were fully committed to Him (2 Chron. 16:9). God was with them. Which, by definition, means He was not with the enemy.

Jehoshaphat responded to the Lord, and the people followed their king's leadership in a beautiful act of honor toward God:

> Then King Jehoshaphat bowed low with his face to the ground. And all the people of Judah and Jerusalem did the same,

> worshiping the Lord. Then the Levites from the clans of Kohath and Korah stood to praise the Lord, the God of Israel, with a very loud shout.
>
> — 2 Chronicles 20:18–19, NLT

This was no ordinary shout; it was a shout of victory to the Lord. It was a shout of verbal agreement that God's words were true, and He was faithful to do what He said He would do. It was full of faith, triumph, and celebration, just as David described in Psalm 47:1: "Shout unto God with the voice of triumph" (KJV).

Early the next morning Judah's army went out toward the battleground as God had directed. Jehoshaphat said, "Listen to me, all you people of Judah and Jerusalem! Believe in the Lord your God, and you will be able to stand firm. Believe in his prophets, and you will succeed" (2 Chron. 20:20 NLT).

If they believed God and His Word—if they remained loyal to God, unwavering in uncertain circumstances—Jehoshaphat encouraged the people they would be able to follow through on God's instructions and stand firm against their enemies.

Praise – God's Ambush

Jehoshaphat positioned singers and worshippers in front of the battle procession to praise the Lord. He believed God would do what He said and was honoring Him with praise before it happened. Jehoshaphat understood that the moment God spoke His instruction it was already completed. He trusted God, who does not lie or change His mind, knowing He would make good on the words He spoke (Num. 23:18–19 NKJV).

Jehoshaphat's trust in God's character enabled him to celebrate the victory that had been released in the unseen realm even before it manifested in the natural realm on the battlefield. Like David, Jehoshaphat could declare, "Give thanks to the Lord, for he is good! His faithful love endures forever" (1 Chron. 16:34 NLT).

The character of God is faithful love. In the story of Jehoshaphat, this faithful love was toward God's people, and it would endure forever no matter what they faced.

Praise is a declaration of the Lord's awesome and glorious character. Thanksgiving is the appreciation of that character, and what it accomplishes. Psalm 22:3 says, "God inhabits the praises of His people" (NKJV). The word "inhabit" is the Hebrew word *yashab* (*Strong's* H3427) and means, "to sit down within as judge in ambush and quiet; to dwell and remain; to lurk." God had already promised He was with Judah. He had already chosen sides. He was dwelling within "the praises of His people" waiting to release judgment against Israel's enemies:

> As they began to sing and praise, the Lord set ambushes against the men of Ammon and Moab and Mount Seir who were invading Judah, and they were defeated. The Ammonites and Moabites rose up against the men from Mount Seir to destroy and annihilate them. After they finished slaughtering the men from Seir, they helped to destroy one another.
>
> When the men of Judah came to the place that overlooks the desert and looked toward the vast army, they saw only dead bodies lying on the ground; no one had escaped. So, Jehoshaphat and his men went to carry off their plunder, and they found among them a great amount of equipment and clothing and articles of value—more than they could take away. There was so much plunder that it took three days to collect it. On the fourth day they assembled in the Valley of Berakah, where they praised the Lord. This is why it is called the Valley of Berakah to this day.
>
> Then, led by Jehoshaphat, all the men of Judah and Jerusalem returned joyfully to Jerusalem, for the Lord had given them cause to rejoice over their enemies. They entered Jerusalem and went to the temple of the Lord with harps and lyres and trumpets.

> The fear of God came on all the surrounding kingdoms when they heard how the Lord had fought against the enemies of Israel. And the kingdom of Jehoshaphat was at peace, for his God had given him rest on every side.
>
> — 2 Chronicles 20:22–30, NIV

The battle was already won, but judgement was not released until the people began to worship the Lord, trusting Him for what He had promised. Praise is what God uses to "ambush" His enemies. Jehoshaphat and Israel learned what it meant to believe God and stand firm until God's love and promises manifested in victory.

From Double-Minded to Single-Minded

God is love and wants what is right and holy for you. His commandments are where the culture of heaven collides with earth. When you act on His instructions, kingdom culture is manifested on earth as it is in heaven, reflecting the heart of the true King of the kingdom. The transformation of Jehoshaphat's kingdom reflected what was going on in his heart.

Jehoshaphat was a man devoted to God. He went from being double-minded and divided in loyalty to being single-minded. He and his people believed God and stood firm. This is a man who became like a nail in a sure place: unwavering. In doing so, God was glorified. His people were exalted above their enemies, they reaped the spoils, and they enjoyed great peace as a nation.

God's mercy to you is no different than His mercy to Jehoshaphat and the people of Judah. You will have times when your loyalty to God is divided, when your mind and heart sways back and forth like the waves of the sea. But like Jehoshaphat, God sees both the good and the bad in you. In His mercy and loving faithfulness, He looks past the bad. However, this place of division in loyalty is not where He wants you to remain. He longs for you to trust Him for what you cannot see, to rejoice in the victory He has already won, and to worship Him through praise that He might release righteous judgment on His enemies.

A Nail in a Sure Place

The phrase "a nail in a sure place" which is woven throughout this book comes from a beautiful passage written by the prophet Isaiah:

> And the key of the house of David will I lay upon his shoulder; so he shall open, and none shall shut; and he shall shut, and none shall open. *And I will fasten him as a nail in a sure place*; and he shall be for a glorious throne to his father's house. And they shall hang upon him all the glory of his father's house, the offspring and the issue, all vessels of small quantity, from the vessels of cups, even to all the vessels of flagons."
>
> — Isaiah 22:22–24, KJV, emphasis added

The word "sure" in Isaiah 22:23 is the same word *aman,* meaning "to believe" is defined as: firm, fixed, committed, established, trust, trustworthy, and fidelity. Some translations use the word "firm," but it is still *aman.* It is God who drives the believer into a "sure" place. But what is that sure place? What is God driving or fastening in the believer into?

God used the word *aman* in Isaiah 22:22–24 as a word picture. In ancient times, stakes were driven into the timbers or fastened and secured into the mortar/concrete of a home. These stakes were permanent, and they could not be moved. They were so steadfast and immovable that they could bear extreme burdens without budging or coming loose. A nail could possibly break off at the point where the wall was, but it could never come out of the wall. Those nails were used to glorify and beautify the house. From them, families would hang decorations, useful vessels, armor, shields, and swords from previous glorious battles.

In the same way, God drives or fastens followers of Jesus like a nail in a sure place. The nail is strong, but it is what the nail is fastened into that allows it to withstand great pressure and not break loose or drop what it is holding. The peg is useless unless it is fastened to something steadfast and immovable— something trustworthy. The Lord and His character is that sure place. The nail—the believer—does not need to do a thing but rest in the mortar or beam of God's unfailing character and love.

On Display for the World to See

When God drives you into His character and you become steadfast, battle glories and other evidence of His goodness and faithfulness will be displayed in your life for all to see. The glory of your Father's house can "hang" off you as you rest in the powerful beam of His character. That word "glory" is Hebrew for *kabowd* (Strong's H3519). *Kabowd* means, "goodness and excellence of character splendor, weighty and honor." The more God "hangs" off you, the more people will see His goodness and be drawn to His mercy. He wants to fasten or drive you into the revelation of His character so that no matter how weighty the things are that God hangs from you; you will be able to display them. He longs to drive you into Him so that you are not tossed about by every circumstance, wind, doctrine or temptation that blows.

As you believe His promises, you can step out confidently and obey whatever He prompts you to do. As you do, the weighty glory and splendor of the spoils will be hung on you for the world to see. It may be that book He told you to write that becomes a bestseller. Maybe it's obeying Him and sharing Jesus with people who need salvation. Perhaps it means starting that business your faith is prompting you to start. As you rest, fastened into His character, the spoils of obedience and the goodness of God's character will be hung on you.

Trusting God's incredible character will bring inner stillness and peace. Those internal arguments between faith and unbelief will be silenced as you fully rely on God who is committed to bringing His promises in your life to pass.

Like Jehoshaphat, as you trust God, you will become single-minded, steadfast, and victorious—like a nail in a sure place. You will find your King going before you in battle and seeing you through to the winning side.

Reflect with the Holy Spirit

Ask God to guide you into a more steadfast and victorious life as you ponder these questions:

1. What symptoms of double-mindedness have I displayed? Where do I feel tossed about and unsettled? ________________________________
   ____
   ____

2. Have I received Your promises, but spent more time worrying and coming up with internal objections and arguments rather than praying through those promises with thanks and celebration, trusting Your great and glorious character? ________________________________
   ____
   ____

3. Am I willing to sing with praise and thanks on the way to battle? What might this look like? Considering areas of my life You have given direction or promises; how can I praise You right now?______________
   ____
   ____

4. Like Jehoshaphat, is there any area in my life that I need to change and establish upon Your Word? ________________________________
   ____
   ____

5. Are there other thoughts You are bringing to my mind? ___________
   ____
   ____

CHAPTER 2 – BELIEVING WITH AN UNDIVIDED HEART

Give me an undivided heart that I might fear you. – Psalm 86:11

Even the strongest followers of Jesus struggle occasionally in their ability to believe God. One reason for this is because they may not know and understand God's love, character, and what He has given them. But another reason people struggle, is because they have divided hearts clinging to two loyalties or loves.

In this world there are countless people and social media messages that consistently encourage: "You can do it; God is with you. Follow your dreams; they are from God!" And they are right! Daily, I would seek this encouragement to medicate and treat the doubt I was facing. This may be the case with you as well. But if the challenge is rooted in divided loyalty, it cannot be fixed with constant encouragement. The problem that first brought the division is what must be fixed. Once the problem is dealt with, it will be possible to stand firm, believe God, and accomplish your God-given dreams and assignments.

Corrie ten Boom, author of *The Hiding Place,* harbored and saved hundreds of Jews from the Nazis and was then imprisoned herself. She survived and later started a worldwide ministry. Ten Boom once said that her faith was like the little recording device she used for her sermons. When it was broken, she would send the recording device to the manufacturer. It is the same with your faith and your act of believing God. Your belief must be brought to Jesus, the great author and finisher your faith. It is He who gives measures of faith and it is He who can repair what is broken.

Believe in God's Promises

"Believe" is an intense word. How does God define it? Why does it work? Why does a person need belief to be stable? In Hebrew, "believe" is the word *aman*, (*Strong's* H539). Recall that it means, "to be firm, endure, be faithful, fidelity, be true, stand fast, trust, trustworthy, truthfulness, true, certain, sure, establish, steadfast, stand fast and faithfulness." It means, "to commit, be quiet and free from internal arguments or objection," but also to be "morally true and certain." Notice the word "fidelity." Fidelity is a word often used to describe faithfulness in marriage.

Look at each of those words in the definition and break them down in the context of what Jehoshaphat declared to God's people: "Be firm, endure and be faithful with fidelity to God. Don't cheat on Him with doubt or lovers. Give Him your whole heart. Be true to Him, steadfast and trustworthy regarding your view of His character and His ways. Be truthful and faithful to Him by believing and doing what He says. Commit and follow through. Go the distance and let your belief endure through obstacles. Be quiet within yourself and free from internal arguments and objections of doubt. Don't put your trust in something else. When God declares He will do something, He will do it; in the same way, stick with Him with fidelity."

Fidelity with Faithfulness

Two loyalties mean to be devoted to or love two people or two things. It's like having both a spouse *and* a lover. When two people love each other so much that they desire to commit to each other in a deep, intimate, and exclusive way, marriage is the next step. When you come to Jesus, you are entering a covenant. He is faithful to you and like any good husband, He is jealous for you, His bride.

Many new couples start strong, but soon life begins to impact their relationship; bills and responsibilities can affect the couple's interactions. Marital love is meant to deepen beyond the early infatuation stage; commitment starts to take a bigger role than feelings as the couple faces obstacles. But sometimes something else happens. One person in the marriage may start to miss the "zing of the fling" of when they first met. He or she may become vulnerable to other affections. Soon another person may catch their interest and through various chats, smiles, and pleasant words, a shared attraction may be birthed. When that mutual attraction becomes more concrete, one person might take the leap and invite the other to deepen the connection through coffees, then lunches, and perhaps dinners—and soon they will cross the line into something physical. Their hearts may begin to develop an affection that creates a greater and greater attachment. However, "physical adultery" is not where the adultery occurred. The adultery occurred when the heart was led astray by its own desires for the "zing of the fling." James put it this way:

> Temptation comes from our own desires, which entice us and drag us away.
>
> — James 1:14, NLT

Does this person stop loving his or her spouse? Not usually. Often their love is still quite intense. But one spouse's heart has become divided. This is where conflict and instability take root within the adulterer.

A Picture of a Divided Heart

I remember when the Holy Spirit gave me a picture to understand the concept better. Imagine a man in the above scenario. He has a wife whom he loves standing on one side of him and his mistress on the other. Each woman is holding tightly to one of his arms. Each love is pulling him back and forth demanding his commitment and fidelity, making him literally unstable and unable to stand firm; he is at the mercy of both loves. He cannot decide which woman he wants more because he has given himself—his heart and loyalty—to each. He is invested in both.

The insecurity of not being able to decide between two loyalties or loves may motivate you to poll others around you. But polling others will do nothing to safeguard your mind from the constant reasoning. Your love for both loyalties will speak to your thoughts and pull you back and forth. The two loyalties will continually natter at you to choose. This can cause mental torment and obsessive thinking and exhaust you emotionally and physically. Making decisions based on your love for both will lead to confusion, and you will not feel at rest.

Look again at how James explains that the source of instability in faith is divided loyalty between God and the world:

> If you need wisdom, ask our generous God, and he will give it to you. He will not rebuke you for asking. But when you ask him, be sure that your faith is in God alone. Do not waver, for a person with divided loyalty is as unsettled as a wave of the sea that is blown and tossed by the wind. Such people should not expect to receive anything from the Lord. Their loyalty is divided between God and the world, and they are unstable in everything they do.
>
> — James 1:5–8, NLT

Recall that the Greek word "faith" is *pistis*, (*Strong's* G4102) and means in the New Testament exactly what "believe" does in the Old Testament. It means, "persuasion, conviction of the truthfulness of God, reliance upon Him, truth, believe, trust with fidelity." *Strong's Exhaustive Concordance* conveys that faith includes the idea of trust with a holy fervor and is used with the idea of trust or confidence in God and fidelity with faithfulness. It describes the character of a reliable person; an adulterer is not reliable. Bill Johnson echoes this saying, "Bold faith stands on the shoulders of quiet trust." Read James 1:5–8 again. I'll wait.

If your loyalty is divided by loving something else, it can affect your ability to have faith and confidence in God, and to believe Him and trust His faithfulness. When you struggle to believe and trust God with fidelity, you subsequently cannot stand firm and then become storm-tossed and afflicted. You become unstable.

There are times in life when our loyalty can be unknowingly divided. Problems may exist, but we may not realize the source of our problem lies in something we are loving and loyal to other than God. Jeremiah wrote that the heart is deceitfully wicked (Jer. 17:9). However, the good news is that God is not. If the cause of a struggle is not clear, God is willing to reveal the source—*the heart*. The heart is the seat and place of affection and devotion and where God has given each of us a measure of faith. When our heart is divided between God and the world, our faith is divided, too, resulting in a heart tossed to and fro in devotion.

What is the Love of the World?

Have you ever wondered what the "love of the world" means? The best definitions are God's definitions. He is the source of all truth and His wonderful Holy Spirit is always present to lead and guide you into all truth. Only truth can set you free to live the life of love, loyalty, and stability God desires. God defines the love of the world in 1 John, along with a caution for His children:

> Do not love this world nor the things it offers you, for when you love the world, you do not have the love of the Father in you. For the world offers only a craving for physical pleasure, a craving for everything we see, and pride in our achievements and possessions. These are not from the Father but are from this world. And this world is fading away, along with everything that people crave. But anyone who does what pleases God will live forever.
>
> — 1 John 2:15–17, NLT

The love of the world is associated with an antichrist spirit or mindset. The term "anti" in the Greek (*Strong's* G473) can mean both "against" and "in place of." An antichrist spirit is opposite to Christ. It is self-seeking. When Satan wanted to usurp God's throne, he did so out of selfish motive and ambition:

> How you are fallen from heaven, O shining star, son of the morning! You have been thrown down to the earth, you who destroyed the nations of the world. For you said to yourself, "I will ascend to heaven and set my throne above God's stars. I will preside on

> the mountain of the gods far away in the north. I will climb to the highest heavens and be like the Most High."
>
> — Isaiah 14:12, NLT

But Jesus Christ is not like that. Jesus is love and according to 1 Corinthians 13, love is defined as not selfish, boastful, or prideful. Rather, it puts others first. Jesus defined the greatest love as a person's willingness to lay down his or her life for a friend. This is not the "gimme-gimme" attitude of Satan. Satan looked at what he could take, while Jesus looked for what He could give and how He could serve. The apostle Paul offers one of the best descriptions of Jesus:

> Do nothing out of selfish ambition or vain conceit. Rather, in humility value others above yourselves, not looking to your own interests but each of you to the interests of the others. In your relationships with one another, have the same mindset as Christ Jesus: Who, being in very nature God, did not consider equality with God something to be used to his own advantage; rather, he made himself nothing by taking the very nature of a servant, being made in human likeness. And being found in appearance as a man, he humbled himself by becoming obedient to death—even death on a cross!
>
> — Philippians 2:3–8, NIV

Jesus did not look out for His own interests. *He looked out for ours.* He gave up His position and the pride of life to become a humble and obedient servant. He loved God enough to take mankind's place, obeying His Father completely. He did not do this for Himself only but for all people, so that through His obedience, they could become sons and daughters of God and share in His wonderful inheritance (Rom. 8:15–17). Jesus loved people and sought to give them all that He had. Conversely, Satan loved *himself* and sought to seize whatever he could for his personal gain.

No wonder God says that friendship with the world—the spirit of antichrist—is enmity with God, and that whoever wishes to be a friend of the world makes himself an enemy of God (James 4:4). It's because the heart behind it is so opposite to God's. What fellowship has light with darkness? None at all.

Satan tried this on both Eve and Jesus with different results. He tempted Eve to pursue her own sense of godhead and to be like God. Satan deceived her and she was led astray from her simple devotion to the Lord to a "gimme-gimme" mindset:

> But I am afraid that just as Eve was deceived by the serpent's cunning, your minds may somehow be led astray from your sincere and pure devotion to Christ.
>
> — 2 Corinthians 11:3, NIV

Eve was tempted in three ways. This temptation lured her away from loyalty to God to loyalty to herself. This is an antichrist mindset—Eve put things in God's place within her heart. These methods of temptation are at work today and are the same temptations Jesus had to overcome. The website *gotquestions.org* succinctly explains:

> Eve was tempted by the serpent to disobey God and eat the forbidden fruit of the tree of knowledge of good and evil. Eve perceived that the fruit was "good for food," "pleasing to the eye," and "desirable for gaining wisdom" (Gen. 3:6). She coveted the fruit in three ways. First, it was appealing to her appetite. John refers to this as the "lust of the flesh," the desire for that which satisfies any of the physical needs. The fruit was also pleasing or delightful to the eye, that which we see and desire to own or possess. Here is the "lust of the eyes" John refers to. Finally, Eve somehow perceived that the fruit would make her wise, giving her a wisdom beyond her own. Part of Satan's lie was that eating the

fruit would make her "like God, knowing good and evil" (Gen. 3:5).

Satan tempted Jesus with the lust of the flesh, bread for His hunger (Matt. 4:2–3), the lust of the eyes, "all the kingdoms of the world with their splendor" (Matt. 4:8–9), and the pride of life, daring Him to cast Himself from the roof of the Temple in order to prove that He was the Messiah by an ostentatious display of power that was not in the will of God or His plan for the redemption of mankind (Matt. 4:5–6). But Jesus, though He was "tempted in every way, just as we are" (Heb. 4:15), resisted the devil and used the Word of God to ensure victory over him.

Christians have always been, and will always be, lured by the same three temptations Eve and Jesus experienced. Satan doesn't change his methods; he doesn't have to because they continue to be successful. He tempts us with the lust of the flesh—sexual gratification, gluttony, excessive alcohol consumption, and drugs, both legal and illegal, as well as the "deeds of the flesh" about which Paul warned the Galatians, "sexual immorality, impurity, sensuality, idolatry, sorcery, enmity, strife, jealousy, fits of anger, rivalries, dissensions, divisions, envy, drunkenness, orgies, and things like these"

— (Gal. 5:19–21).[2]

Satan tempts people with the lust of the eyes—the endless accumulation of "stuff" with which people fill their homes and garages leading to the insatiable desire for more, better, and newer possessions. These little lovers can ensnare people and harden their hearts to the things of God. The love of the world opposes the love of God; like a mistress, it can tempt and lure a person away from fidelity. It can cause people to become calloused to their first love: Jesus Christ. Soon they begin to act in a manner that is self-seeking and anti-Christ in nature.

---

[2] GotQuestions.org. N.p., 26 May 2017. Web. 30 May 2017.

Boundaries and Obedience

Jesus understood something about relationships that He wanted us, His followers to know and understand. He knew that boundaries are gateways to intimacy and relationship. The strength of love in a relationship is proved when one person honors the other person's value; this is done through boundaries. When boundaries are honored, each person feels trusted and as a result becomes closer to the other party. There are boundaries in every friendship, whether spoken or not.

I have three amazing friends. I met them all at the same time. It was during a strong and fantastic phase in my life. They rallied around me while I was working on a project and I felt like I had found my tribe. We had the same mission, values, and passion for Jesus Christ. But I realized that with those friendships came responsibility. I needed to treasure them. I quickly learned what was important to them and did my utmost to honor and uphold those things. I knew instinctively where their boundaries were with family, time, friendships, and truth, and was careful not to cross those lines. Why? Because my friends may have pulled away if I didn't. Being close with people who do not respect boundaries is difficult.

All of God's ways are right and true, and as a good Father, He has outlined everything needed for a prosperous and wonderful life in the Bible—mapped out for our benefit. His instruction reflects who God is and His great love for us, such as not murdering, stealing, or coveting. When those commands are violated, they hurt the people whom God loves and grieves His Holy Spirit. Treasuring and honoring a person's boundaries cherishes them as a person and honors his or her God-given value. They, in turn, can trust us with a greater measure of their heart because they know they will not be hurt or devalued.

Jesus honored what the Father honored. He revered it and served it with holy awe. Jesus never violated any of God's commands and by doing so communicated clearly that the Father could be close to Him. Jesus encouraged us to abide within His boundaries, so we could remain in His steadfast love:

> As the Father has loved me, so have I loved you. Now remain in my love. If you keep my commands, you will remain in my love, just as I have kept my Father's commands and remain in his love.
>
> — John 15:9, 10, NIV

> Whoever has my commands and keeps them is the one who loves me. The one who loves me will be loved by my Father, and I too will love them and show myself to them.
>
> — John 14:21, NIV

God wants to reveal greater and greater measures of Himself to you. Those greater measures are saved for those who will treasure His heart and value what He values. God can trust those who do not hurt Him or grieve Him. When other loves compete for your affection and devotion, it hurts God's heart and He distances Himself from you. Although He never leaves His children, they might feel less of His presence and fellowship. It is like a parent whose child has been disobedient. The parent hasn't abandoned the child who may be on a "time-out" in his or her room. The parent still loves the child and is fully present nearby, but for a time they are not close. Neither the parent or child are enjoying the full benefits of their relationship.

God sets boundaries to help guard His people against a divided heart, and to reveal deeper measures of Himself.

David Versus Solomon: Two Different Hearts

I remember the day God showed me the different hearts of two of the most famous men in the Bible; King David and King Solomon. David wanted an undivided heart, to be able to go in and out before God. God was his top priority, and as such he begged of God:

> Give me an undivided heart, that I may fear Your name.
>
> — Psalm 86:11, NIV

David was considered a man after God's own heart. He continually meditated on God's ways and treasured them in his heart so that he could obey them with ease. This led to much time in God's presence. David cried out to the Lord in prayerful song:

> Create in me a pure heart, O God, and renew a steadfast spirit within me.
>
> — Psalm 51:10, NIV

That word "steadfast" is similar to "believe." It is the same Hebrew word, *kuwn*, used in 2 Chronicles 17:5 when Scripture says the Lord "established" Jehoshaphat's control over the kingdom of Judah. *Kuwn* (*Strong's* H559) means, "established, fixed, unwavering, render sure, appoint, faithfulness, fasten, firm, ordain, order." Recall that the word "believe" means, "firm, faithful, to be permanent, quiet, establish, steadfast, sure." David knew that a pure heart would be steadfast in belief and would be committed to God with unwavering fidelity. David also knew he would sin sometimes, which is why He also asked God to "renew, put back, and bring back into place, a steadfast spirit within me." Indeed, David made many mistakes and grieved God's Spirit; but God was ready to restore him and renew him just as He does for His people today and just as He did with Jehoshaphat.

David understood that when his heart was aligned with God's he would possess God's character, God's heart, and God's faith. Thus, he delighted in and treasured God's commands and boundaries. The Lord made a covenant with David, promising he would always have a descendant on the throne. This culminated with Jesus taking the *everlasting* throne as the King of kings and the Lord of lords.

God's heart is *never* divided but fully committed to His people with faithfulness and fidelity. David's undivided, faithful heart caused God to proclaim David as "having a heart after His own" (1 Sam. 13:14; Acts 13:22). This undivided heart was what enabled David to know the Lord, perform exploits, lead God's people into a greater knowledge and love of their heavenly Father. He could do this because it is the pure in heart that see God. David went in and out before the Lord and became the greatest king that ever lived because he allowed God to pattern his heart after His own.

Unfortunately, Solomon—David's son—had a different heart. Though he asked God for wisdom, Solomon wanted to go in and out before man, not God. His heart was divided in loyalty:

> Give me now wisdom and knowledge, that I may go out and come in before this people, for who can rule this great people of Yours?
>
> — 2 Chronicles 1:10, NASB

The love of man and worldly enticements led to the breakdown of Solomon's empire. He married foreign wives that wooed him—and ultimately wooed his kingdom—into idolatry that Israel was not able to overcome. Rather, Israel continually vacillated between honoring idols and honoring the Lord.

Solomon wrote the book of Ecclesiastes towards the end of his life, and in it declared the meaninglessness of life (Eccl. 1:2). David, on the other hand, declared the following before he took his last breath:

> Yours, O Lord, is the greatness, the power, the glory, the victory and the majesty. Everything in the heavens and on earth is yours, O Lord, and this is your kingdom. We adore you as the One who is over all things.
>
> — 1 Chronicles 29:11, NLT

Both Solomon and David achieved great things for God, but only one of them *knew* God intimately. David's heart and obedience drew him closer to the Lord as he sought to align his heart with God's.

Shipwrecked . . . or Finishing the Race?

The love of the world will tempt God's people and cause believers to desert Christ if they don't deal with the temptation. When a person's heart—the seat of love and devotion—is divided, his or her faith is divided too because the heart is the place where God deposits faith. It is with the heart a person believes God. Recall that "believe" means "faithful." If part of a person's heart is faithful to the love of the world (sin) and part is faithful to God, he or she will be tossed back and forth between those conflicting devotions like waves on the ocean. Eventually they will be shipwrecked.

In his letter to Timothy, Paul described this kind of situation among his former co-workers in the gospel:

> Timothy, my son, here are my instructions for you, based on the prophetic words spoken about you earlier. May they help you fight well in the Lord's battles. Cling to your faith in Christ, and keep your conscience clear. For some people have deliberately violated their consciences; as a result, their faith has been shipwrecked. Hymenaeus and Alexander are two examples.
>
> — 1 Timothy 1:18, NLT

Paul, Timothy's father in the faith, instructed Timothy to wage battle with the prophetic Word and cling to his faith in the Lord. However, he issued a warning to Timothy to keep his conscience clear at the same time, because loving both God and the world means cheating on God. Cheating can never be done with a clear conscience; followers of Jesus must remain devoted and strive to keep their hearts pure, turning from the temptation of another mistress.

Paul wrote to Timothy again in another letter, grieved by the same situation with yet another servant of Christ:

> Timothy, come as soon as you can for Demas has deserted me, having loved this present world, and has departed for Thessalonica.
>
> — 2 Timothy 4:9–10, NLT

Paul cried out for his true and faithful son. True sons do not depart from their father's mission. They love their father and stay the course. Demas struggled with a divided heart and this division pulled him away from God, Paul, and his

destiny. The writer of Hebrews entreated God's faithful people to take Him and His plan seriously by aggressively throwing off sin to be able to faithfully finish the race set before them:
Faith comes from hearing God. A faithful, undivided heart devoted to God will enable a person to act on what he or she heard from Him in a steadfast, established, and confident way and will not be pulled off course by a mistress vying for their attention. Just as a mistress hardens a man's heart toward his wife and prevents him from fulfilling his marital commitment, so sin hardens our heart toward God, making it difficult for us to finish our commitment to Him. This resistance can lead to rebellion that will hinder them from being obedient to God. The writer of Hebrews puts it this way:

> You must warn each other every day, while it is still "today," so that none of you will be deceived by sin and hardened against God. And to whom did God swear that they would never enter his rest if not to those who disobeyed? So we see that they were not able to enter, because of their unbelief.
>
> — Hebrews 3:13, 18–19, NLT

Obedience keeps our hearts undivided and soft, beating in time with God's heart. It enables you to fully access the incredible deposit of faith God has given you to live out your assignments—and to receive the blessings He is waiting to pour out. Interestingly, the Greek word "unbelief" in Hebrews 3:19 is *apaistia* (*Strong's* G570) meaning, "unfaithfulness in action and disobedience." It means being unfaithful in action to the word God speaks to a person's heart. If unbelief means disobedience, then faith means obedience—faithfulness with fidelity to the Word.

A Lesson from Ancient Saints

The greatest and most powerful passage on faith is Hebrews 11, deemed "the faith chapter." With the understanding that faith is obedience, inserting the word "obedience" in place of "faith" in Hebrews 11 illuminates a deeper perspective.

God led each person listed in Hebrews 11. That's why believers are called "followers"—because they follow God's lead out of obedience. These heroes of faith possessed hearts that believed God was good. They repented when they blew it, and allowed God to renew a right and steadfast heart and spirit within them. Even though many of them made mistakes, just as believers do today, heaven and earth recorded their faith—their obedience.

Reflect on just a few of the verses in Hebrews 11 that shed light and understanding of the word "faith" by using the *other* word—obedience—as its definition:

> Now *obedience* is the substance of things confidently trusted for, the evidence of things not seen. For by it the elders obtained a good testimony.
> By *obedience* Abel offered to God a more excellent sacrifice than Cain, through which he obtained witness that he was righteous, God testifying of his gifts; and through it he being dead still speaks. By *obedience* Enoch was taken away so that he did not see death, "and was not found, because God had taken him . . . before he was taken he was commended as having pleased God" (Heb. 11:15 ESV). But without *obedience* it is impossible to please Him, for he who comes to God must believe that He is, and that He is a rewarder of those who diligently seek Him. By *obedience* Noah, being divinely warned of things not yet seen, moved with godly fear, prepared an ark for the saving of his household, by which he condemned the world and became heir of the righteousness which is according to obedience. By *obedience* Abraham obeyed when he was called to go out to the place which he would receive as an inheritance. And he went out, not knowing where he was going.
> By *obedience* they passed through the Red Sea as by dry land, whereas the Egyptians, attempting to do so, were drowned. By

> *obedience* the walls of Jericho fell down after they were encircled for seven days.
>
> — Hebrews 11:1, 4–8, 29–30, emphasis added, ESV

As you begin to unburden yourself of the noisy mistress of sin and the love of the world tempting you away from your first love, you will experience peace mentally and emotionally and be able to follow only one voice: your Shepherd, Jesus Christ. Cultivating an undivided loyalty for the Lord will enable you to stand firm and become like a nail in a sure place in your faith. In obedience, you will be able to walk out your God-given assignments, just as Jehoshaphat did.

Reflect with the Holy Spirit

Invite the Holy Spirit to speak to you and help you see what may be keeping you from becoming a nail in a sure place. Use the questions below as prompts to help you see anything that may be causing division in your heart. He is the Spirit of truth, comfort and love.

1. Lord, are there any mistresses vying for my heart? ________________

   ____

   ____

2. Are there any boundaries I am crossing that You would like to discuss?

   ____

   ____

3. Show me how You feel when I keep Your boundaries. ______________

   ____

   ____

4. Is there anything in my life violating my conscience? Is there anything I have changed in my life that is giving me peace and that brings You delight? ____

____

____

5. Is there anything else You would like to ponder with me? __________

____

____

Chapter 3 – The Lusts of the Flesh

Create in me a clean heart, O God and renew a steadfast spirit within me.
— Psalm 51:10

For most of my life I had struggled with a love for food. I remember being a teenager and buying several Mars bars and going into the school bathroom to hide while I ate them. I knew that eating Mars bars was not wrong and no one would condemn me for eating them. It was *how many* I ate and *how badly* I wanted them that was the problem. I had certain friends that I could eat with who did not mind me pounding back a huge bag of chips, old-fashioned donuts, and chocolate. In fact, they were happy to enjoy those treats with me. But I often felt guilty or uncomfortable with myself after.

For years, I would be confused when I would offer people a brownie or some other snack and they would say, "No, thank you. I'm not hungry." I can honestly remember the day I thought "What does that have to do with anything?" It did not matter to me if I was hungry or not. It was the pleasure, enjoyment, and satisfaction that food offered that drew me, not the hunger. My weight would go up and down. I spent a great deal of time thinking about food—planning what I was going to eat, longing for food, and thinking of my next meal. This continued for years.

I began to experiment with bulimia, making myself sick after eating to get rid of the food—but I felt terrible after doing this, too. It was at this point I began to sense something was wrong. I remember praying and asking God for help but did not sense any freedom. I phoned my father and confessed what was happening. He prayed with me, but again I did not sense any freedom. It was as if there was a noose around my neck, not tight enough to choke the life out of me, but tight enough that I could not get free.

I had always enjoyed God's presence and my prayer times were filled with joy, love, and tears that came in intimate and close moments. What moved His heart moved mine and I enjoyed Him. But I had hit a wall and I could not grow closer to Him. It was as though my prayers went up to heaven, hit a brass ceiling, and fell back to the earth. I couldn't understand what was happening and found myself continually questioning God.

As my questioning continued, I decided to go down to the local Christian bookstore. I enjoyed the sense of God's presence that rested in the store as I wandered through the aisles. I found a book for a friend that was going through a devastating time. But right beside that book was another book by John Bevere. I pulled the book off the shelf and flipped it over to read the back cover, only to find the question: "Do the heavens feel like brass?" It was the exact phrase that had been filling my mind! I quickly paid for the book with the expectation that through its pages God would reveal the mystery of His distance.

That night I took my book to bed and began to read. After only a few pages the Lord released an understanding into my mind and my heart. His distance was because of my love for food. I had no idea the two were related! I had wounded Him and myself, and the realization made me cry. My heart agreed with His word. I repented and confessed to God with a complete brokenness, "I love food more than You." I rolled onto my side, wept, and fell asleep.

It was three days before I realized there had been a change: *I had not thought about food for three days.* I had a new clarity and quietness of mind. I had only eaten when I was hungry and stopped when I was full. By the time Sunday rolled around, as I dressed for church, I realized I had already lost weight and it had not even been on my mind. A new joy welled up inside me. My love for Jesus had returned and we were in great communication. The joy was so vast that I stood up to testify at church what God had done in my life. The joy of Jesus' love went through our congregation with celebration. Within two-and-a-half months, I lost fifty pounds.

Some may call that much weight loss in such little time unhealthy, but I simply ate when my body called for fuel and stopped when I felt the first bite or two of fullness. This is God's glorious mechanism for the human body to manage and fuel itself. God builds everything well, including the human body. His yoke was easy for me, and His burden was light. The truth is simple, but people complicate it with divided loyalties; they don't see the benefit of living in the truth when they want something else more. My heart had been divided, my loyalty split between God and food. But God healed my divided heart and brought me to victory through repentance and eating His way.

The Lord has given all of Himself in an unfathomable way. He withheld nothing, including His Son, who also holds nothing back from those He loves. When a person enters a relationship with Jesus, he or she enters a relationship with someone whose love cannot be measured because it is eternal. The one who loves more is wounded more when that love is shared with an outside third party. I was looking to a third party named "food" for fulfillment, pleasure, joy, and satisfaction—*the definition of adultery*. Like Eve, I had been tempted with the promise of something I already had, and away from pure and simple devotion to Christ. However, only in God's presence did I find fullness of joy.

Cutting Off Temptation

Jesus warned against a split in devotion, saying, "No one can serve two masters. Either he will hate the one and love the other, or he will be devoted to the one and despise the other" (Matt. 6:24).

Submitting to God and using the sword of God's Word was the Lord's antidote for me, and it is the antidote for all believers:

> Therefore, submit to God. Resist the devil and he will flee from you. Draw near to God and He will draw near to you.
>
> — James 4:7-8, NKJV

Remember that Jesus used the Word to resist Satan in the wilderness and cut off the second head of temptation that would natter at Him to lead him out of His loyalty to His Father.

> For the word of God is living and active, sharper than any two-edged sword, piercing to the division of soul and of spirit, of joints and of marrow, and discerning the thoughts and intentions of the heart.
>
> — Hebrews 4:12, NASB

The Word of God works the same for believers today as it did with Jesus in the first century. Satan may tempt a person to enjoy one more helping of food, one extra glass of wine, or one little look at that good-looking person. He may entice someone to view just a little bit of sex, take that pain killer to relax, or spend extra time sleeping beyond what is needed. He will lure people to make a little more money or tell a small lie to reach a goal. He will even use things like video streaming services and social media to lure people into laziness.

Indulgence in the flesh begins after the point of "enough." It will start small and seem harmless at first. It will begin to divide your heart just a little. But Jesus is not content to have part of your heart. He wants your whole heart and will pursue it. Satan knows He needs only a bit to divide and compromise your faith and create doubt in God, which could prevent you from fulfilling your God-given assignments with peace, confidence and joy.

Satan's best tactic is making a person think something is good and will satisfy his or her desires. In reality, God says:

> Do not be deceived, my beloved brethren. Every good gift and every perfect gift is from above, and comes down from the Father of lights, with whom there is no variation or shadow of turning.
>
> — James 1:16-17, ESV

Resist the lies of the enemy. God's plan and the joy of peace that comes from trusting Him are better than anything Satan can offer. Satan's lies are insidious traps against every incredible opportunity God gives you to be an answer to the lost people in this world. Your heart holds within it the ability to believe God and His Word—to look at mountains and say with confidence, "Get out of my way and be cast into the sea. You have no business here!" and know it will be done.

God is Ready to Unite Your Heart

One day I was listening to the Lord and He told me something: "Would I have crucified my Son if I did not truly *want* to forgive and restore my children? Was I only half-hearted in my desire and my decision? Yet my children are afraid to come. They think I won't want to forgive them, that they must wrestle it out of me. I delight to forgive them and renew a right and steadfast spirit within them."

Perhaps, like my experience with food, you can no longer continue down the path of sin. Your Savior is mighty to save; He came to destroy the works of the devil (1 John 3:18). If it's tough right now, you are a perfect candidate for the goodness of God in Jesus Christ and the power of the Holy Spirit to break that loyalty to the lust of the flesh in your life. The Holy Spirit is with you, ready to highlight sin to confess. Let Him come and speak. He is the Spirit of the Father in heaven who is pleased to be with you and unite your heart and make it one again. He takes no pleasure in making you feel condemned or miserable and unworthy. Rather, God's Word says He will restore your soul and will lead you in paths of righteousness for His name's sake (Psalm 23:3). He longs to forgive . . . forgiveness is who He is.

You are here to change the landscape of this world to match the landscape of heaven—and there is no greater joy in life! However, it will take undivided faith from an undivided heart to jump into the unknown. If you are ready to jump, know that in the invisible spiritual realm, the arms of your trustworthy Father are waiting to catch you as you *believe*. Do not share your heart with His enemy. Keep it for Jesus alone. Wholeheartedly His!

Reflect with the Holy Spirit

Ask the Lord to shine His light in your heart, and to give you the strength and grace to see what He is waiting to reveal, and deal with it. Spend time writing out your thoughts to the questions below or sit quietly before Him and confess anything that comes to mind that might be dividing your heart. He delights to forgive and bring freedom.

1. Lord, how are You pursuing my whole heart right now? ____________

   ____

   ____

2. How is the enemy pursuing even a small bit of my heart? __________

   ____

   ____

3. What words or sword of the Spirit do I need to use to cut off the second head? ____

   ____

   ____

4. When I cut off the second head, what does this do to Your heart as my God and first love? ______________________________

   ____

   ____

5. Am I experiencing more peace with less natter pulling me in different directions? More? ______________________________

   ____

   ____

CHAPTER 4 – GOD'S STRENGTH ALONE

Remember, dear brothers and sisters, that few of you were wise in the world's eyes or powerful or wealthy when God called you.
— 1 Corinthians 1:26, NLT

Amy Carmichael once said, "When the heart learns to trust God as He should be trusted, utterly and without hesitation, then the Lord throws wide the door of the treasure house of grace, and bids us go in with boldness and receive our inheritance of the saints in the light."

Though even the strongest believers know this to be true, there are many things that will compete for a person's attention and subtly woo him or her to trust in themselves and their own strength, rather than trusting in God.

The Pride of Life

When I made the decision to follow God's leading into ministry, I was beyond excited. But as I studied in preparation, I watched everyone else's life around me change in what looked like a more secure way than mine. They began to pursue degrees and move into positions. I began to feel inferior as the achievements of others mounted around me; without realizing it, I had begun to walk by sight and not by faith. I noticed something else had changed—my speech. Out of insecurity, I began to speak more highly of myself than I ought. I had believed a lie, and the only antidote to a lie is the truth. God has no greater joy than when His children walk in truth (3 John 1:4). Sadly, I had said "yes" to the Lord, but did not fully trust He would bring His calling on my life to fruitfulness. But His remedy was on the way and so is yours.

One day the Lord led me to the following verses to end my internal conflict:

> Brothers and sisters, think of what you were when you were called. Not many of you were wise by human standards; not many were influential; not many were of noble birth. But God chose the foolish things of the world to shame the wise; God chose the weak things of the world to shame the strong. God chose the lowly things of this world and the despised things—and the things that are not—to nullify the things that are, so that no one may boast before him.
>
> — 1 Corinthians 1:26–29, NIV

I heard the Lord speak to me quietly, "I chose you and called you when you were not wise or powerful and had no remarkable status. I chose you and appointed you from the state you were in to bear fruit. Why do you feel like you need to be more to prove that I called you?"

The pressure was off. I did not need to qualify God's choice and approval. I did not have to audition for my calling—it was God-given. God sent me to preach the gospel, not to prove myself worthy to others. I was going after the world's value system of status and recognition to fill my need for security, when I was secure all along. I was leaning on and trusting the world's value system for strength, rather than trusting in the authority God had already given me. The moment I trusted my life into His hands, I was secure, and so are you.

The "pride of life" will vie for our attention. It attempts to measure a person's value by achievements, status, and power. Enjoying a blessed life after working hard and being rewarded is great. It's God's blessing for His children to eat and drink and enjoy good labor (Eccl. 3:13). God does not want His children to possess mindsets where they exalt themselves in their own sight wherein they boast in worldly wisdom, status, or self-effort; He does not want them to think more highly of themselves than they ought in a self-promoting manner.

Sometimes people do this because they feel insecure and are inclined to want to be "enough," to have value in society, and to feel they belong or are worthy. People measure themselves by their peer's value system, thinking it will make them feel safe, secure, worthy, or successful. Unfortunately, people's value systems constantly change, even from one person to the next.

Imagine being on the ocean and trying to swim to the top of a peaked wave; just when you think you are at the top, the wave falls, but soon there is another peaked wave to ascend. The waves come constantly, one on top of the other, and they are all surrounding. The world is an uncertain ocean of opinion, void of stability. You will never remain above the wave you are trying to ascend. *Seeking peace based on our own performance will result in a life that constantly swells up and down.* It will contribute to a divided heart and keep you from experiencing God's joy and peace. God's value system, however, never changes.

God wants to unfold His power and fruitfulness through us and all believers whom He sends into their God given destinies simply because He loves us and enjoys working in partnership with us, His sons and daughters.

Delegated Authority: The Principle of Being Sent

The Bible tells a story about a centurion, who interestingly was not commended for faith in Christ! Rather, he was commended for his faith *in the authority of God, who sent Jesus*:

> When Jesus had entered Capernaum, a centurion came to him, asking for help. "Lord," he said, "my servant lies at home paralyzed, suffering terribly." Jesus said to him, "Shall I come and heal him?" The centurion replied, "Lord, I do not deserve to have you come under my roof. But just say the word, and my servant will be healed. For I myself am a man under authority, with soldiers under me. I tell this one, 'Go,' and he goes; and that one, 'Come,' and he comes. I say to my servant, 'Do this,' and he does it." When Jesus heard this, he was amazed and said to those following him, "Truly I tell you, I have not found anyone in Israel with such great faith. I say to you that many will come from the east and the west, and will take their places at the feast with Abraham, Isaac, and

> Jacob in the kingdom of heaven. But the subjects of the kingdom will be thrown outside, into the darkness, where there will be weeping and gnashing of teeth." Then Jesus said to the centurion, "Go! Let it be done just as you believed it would." And his servant was healed at that moment.
>
> — Matthew 8:6–13, NIV

The centurion, a military man, understood that the person who acted at the command and commission of his superior had the same but delegated authority as the superior himself. When a general of the US military is in the Middle East and is issued a command, for example, he acts not on his own authority but on the authority of the president. In addition, the president affords him the strength and military might to execute the command.

When God asks a person to complete an assignment for Him on the earth, His strength and power will be present to make it a living reality through that person's obedience. His strength and power are also keys to salvation and accessing the benefits of Jesus' assignments. The "subjects of the kingdom" in Matthew 8:6–13 were cast out of God's kingdom because they did not perceive God had sent Jesus into the world (John 3:16). John wrote even the Jews, Jesus' own people, didn't recognize or receive Him:

> He came to His own, and those who were His own did not receive Him. But as many as received Him, to them He gave the right to become children of God.
>
> — John 1:11–12, NASB

It is up to those to whom you are sent to receive and access the blessings within your assignments. As you step forward, God does not ask you to rely on your own strength, but on the delegated authority of God and the power of the Holy Spirit He has given you. And, like the general of the United States who has access to the president's storehouses of authority and resources, *you* have access to God's heavenly storehouses of resources for all you need. Expect God to release His power, strength, and miracles just like He did for His seventy-two disciples when He sent them out:

> After this the Lord appointed seventy-two others and sent them two by two ahead of him to every town and place where he was about to go. "Whoever listens to you listens to me; whoever rejects you rejects me; but whoever rejects me rejects him who sent me." The seventy-two returned with joy and said, "Lord, even the demons submit to us in Your name." He replied, "I saw Satan fall like lightning from heaven. I have given you authority to trample on snakes and scorpions and to overcome all the power of the enemy; nothing will harm you. However, do not rejoice that the spirits submit to you, but rejoice that your names are written in heaven."
>
> — Luke 10:1, 16–20, NIV

Notice the principle of being sent in the above verses. The power and authority to execute the assignment was within the Lord's command. The seventy-two were not acting on their own authority, but God's. God sent Jesus and Jesus had the right and authority to send the disciples; He did, and He still does today. Begin to trust and believe that God will supernaturally supply the strength, power, wisdom, organization, or miracles for any assignment He gives you.

Loaves and A Lake

The disciples received two assignments from Jesus that seemed unrelated. However, Jesus connected them so that believers will understand what happens when they obey—and how to apply those examples to any God-given assignments with a soft and believing heart.

The First Assignment: The Loaves

Jesus, despite His human fatigue, had compassion for the people and showed Himself as the exact representation of the Father by teaching and instructing the people and healing the sick. But the next need was before Him: *hunger*. The disciples begged Jesus to send the crowd away to get their own food, but good fathers feed their kids. Jesus' work was not yet complete.

Jesus needed to represent the Father again to the crowd, but He also in turn needed to teach His disciples how to represent Him and His Father to the world. So, He told the disciples, "You give them something to eat" (Matt. 14:16 NIV). The disciples had just seen God—through Jesus and then through them—do the miraculous, and they were incredulous. They had spent much time with Jesus but still didn't understand that Jesus only did what He saw His Father doing, and it always worked out—even during trials.

The disciples began to look at their own strengths and abilities for this colossal God-sized task, saying, "We'd have to work for months to earn enough money to buy food for all these people" (Mark 6:37 NLT). And that is exactly the point. Jesus asked them to gather what food they could and bring it to Him. With five loaves and two fish, they were about to represent the Father in the power of delegated authority.

Jesus began to show them how. He did not look at the crowd or at His disciples for guidance, but to His Father who spoke to His heart: "Feed them." He lifted the loaves and fish and gave thanks to the Father for His provision even before it arrived. He knew God supplied His power for His commands and will to be done on the earth. Jesus broke off some food and gave it to the disciples; food multiplied at His hands and at the disciples' hands, and Scripture says, "they did all eat and were filled" (Matt. 14:20 KJV). The Greek word for "filled" is *chortazo,* (*Strong's* H5526) which means, "to gorge, feed abundantly and full"—much like an enormous Thanksgiving dinner with abundant leftovers.

Now that's the kingdom of God coming on earth as it is in heaven. There's always an abundance in the Father's house. He's the Everlasting God, the King of the universe—and kings put on banquets. It is not the servant's responsibility to pay for the food, only to serve it at the king's orders. God is the Father King and He feeds His kids.

Followers of Jesus will experience unspeakable joy when they participate in miracles by responding in obedience to the King's requests. His strength, power, and resources are released into His assignments with abundance.

The Second Assignment: The Lake

At the end of that same day, Jesus gave His disciples a second assignment: to cross the lake to Bethsaida. So, they begin rowing across the lake while Jesus was in prayer on the mountain. Halfway across the lake, a storm began. The contrary wind was howling, throwing waves into the boat, and rowing was nearly futile. The fourth watch of the night approached—between 3:00 a.m. and 6:00 a.m. The disciples were already exhausted from the previous day's ministry journey and from feeding the crowds, and now they were physically spent from rowing all night. Suddenly, they saw Jesus walking on the water in the middle of the storm. Mark's version adds just a bit of interesting information: "He was about to pass by them" (Mark 6:48 NIV). Jesus intended to walk past His terrified friends—which seems peculiar. However, don't forget: *Jesus only did what He saw His Father doing.*

A Failed Test and Hard Hearts

Jesus passed by His disciples because the Father was testing them in their understanding of the lesson learned in the assignment of feeding the five thousand. Look at the parallel passage from Mark's viewpoint:

> He saw that they were in serious trouble, rowing hard and struggling against the wind and waves. About three o'clock in the morning Jesus came toward them, walking on the water. He intended to go past them, but when they saw him walking on the water, they cried out in terror, thinking he was a ghost. They were all terrified when they saw him.
> But Jesus spoke to them at once. "Don't be afraid," he said. "Take courage! I am here!" Then he climbed into the boat, and the wind stopped. They were totally amazed, ***for they still didn't***

> ***understand the significance of the miracle of the loaves. Their hearts were too hard to take it in.***
>
> —Mark 6:48-52, NLT, emphasis added

Although they didn't pass the test, it exposed something within them that led to the failure. The disciples needed to learn God's strength would accomplish every task He gave; how quickly they forgot what happened when Jesus commanded them to feed the multitude with the bread and the fish! They only needed to respond in obedience.

When Jesus sent His disciples to the other side of the lake, His same power was available in the command to "go" as it was to feed the multitude. They could have spoken to the wind and the waves or any obstacle in their path. God's Word and command in their mouth was just as powerful as Jesus' own command in His mouth—just as with the centurion who said, "Just say the word and my servant will be healed."

Later, after Jesus rose from the dead, He appeared to His disciples and sent them with a fresh mandate and an infilling of the Holy Spirit because He would not physically be with them anymore. Jesus said:

> As the Father has sent Me, I also send you. And when He had said this, He breathed on them and said to them, "Receive the Holy Spirit."
>
> — John 20:21, NASB

In each assignment, Jesus represented the Father on earth as the exact representation of His being. Just as the Father supplied Jesus with the Holy Spirit, Jesus supplies you. That Person, the Holy Spirit, is all you need. Trust Him and obey even when it seems Jesus is walking past you. It is a sign He trusts you to address your obstacles with His authority.

Fight against allowing your heart to become hardened with unbelief when the test or trial comes. Hardness of heart comes when the believer looks to two loyalties for strength—Jesus, and self. Only one is God! You cannot trust in yourself and God at the same time. When you trust in your own strength, a war will rage within you because you, more than anyone else, know your weaknesses. One part of your heart will tell you to trust in the Lord, and the other will tell you to trust in yourself. These two nattering heads arguing back and forth will try to convince you which way to lean. Subconsciously, you know you cannot handle everything; often, anxiety will ensue.

Trusting in self is a pride of life and a love of the world. It clings to this world and is a self-focused means of handling life, ultimately trusting in one's own strength rather than God's. It will pull a person away from loyalty to God and submitting to Him out of joyful obedience.

Your *Real* Authority, Power, and Status

Satan is an expert at tempting those God calls into believing that they do not actually have what they possessed since becoming a child of God. Satan did the same thing to Eve, tempting her to eat the apple because it would exalt her in wisdom and make her like God when she already had access to the Godhead every day. Paul wrote that within this Godhead are "all the treasures of wisdom and knowledge" (Col. 2:3 NLT).

Eve could have asked God anything she wanted to know. He would have been pleased to bless her with understanding. Because she was made in His image, she was already "like" God (Gen. 1:27). That word "image" in Hebrew is *tselem*, (*Strong's* H6754) which means, "phantom, illusion, resemblance, a representative figure." Dutch Sheets, author of the book *Intercessory Prayer*, explained *tselem* to mean that creation did a double–take when Eve walked by; she and Adam were so much in God's image that at first glance all of creation would have thought it was God. But upon further and closer inspection, they would have realized it was Adam or Eve.

Notice that image (*tselem*) defined Eve as a representative figure. Just as God had governing authority and power over creation, so did she. Eve was to represent God and His authority in her rule and dominion of the earth. Satan will try to convince God's people that they don't have enough, when they have something *greater* than power: God's governing authority. Authority is the right to exercise power. Recall that God has assigned and given the earth to man (Psalm 115:16), not Satan. This means that when God gives a man or woman an assignment, he or she has the right to use His authority and power to complete the task. Christians have complete authority over Satan's limited power. Jesus declared what this power and authority should look like in a believer's life:

> Behold, I give you the authority to trample on serpents and scorpions, and over *all* the power of the enemy, and nothing shall by any means hurt you.
>
> — Luke 10:19, NKJV, emphasis added

The word authority is *exousia* (Strong's G1849) which means, "jurisdiction, magistrate, right and superhuman." The word power is *dunamis* (Strong's G 1411) which means "miraculous power." Jesus is saying, "I have given you jurisdiction, magistrate and superhuman strength over all the miraculous power of the devil". Satan must be put in his place through binding and rebuking him, prayer and by speaking the truth of the Word of God—and God will expand a person's influence as they use their authority and power wisely and faithfully. Satan will tempt believers to take that power or authority for themselves or to believe that they do not have any to begin with. *Don't let these strategic attacks cause a sense of insecurity that will slip into chasing earthly status and power.*

Those who love the world and chase this false sense of status and power give their hearts to a counterfeit lover, but Satan offers nothing of real value. You already have what is of the highest value; it's real and God has given it to you for serving the world and Jesus. Remember who you are—a powerful person of God created in His image to govern the earth. What higher status is there than that? What higher power can a person have?

Serve God, Not the World

When God created Adam and Eve it was because He wanted to love them. Their gifts and talents were part of God's plan for their lives. He gave them the assignments to subdue the earth, fill it and to multiply all He had given them using those very same gifts and talents. They were to govern the earth, representing or "re-presenting" Him by bringing the culture and ways of the kingdom of God and its King to earth. It was a task so vast and so great that was to be handed down from generation to generation until Jesus returns to rule and reign from Jerusalem. Utilizing the gifts God gives is part of that plan.

Upon creation, God looked at Adam and Eve in wonder. The Word says that they were "fearfully and wonderfully made." The word "fearfully" is the Hebrew word *yare* (*Strong's* H3372). It means, "to fear, morally, to revere, reverence, and awe, dread as in powerful." It is the same word David used to describe God in Psalm 33:8 saying, "Let all the earth fear [*yare'*] the Lord; let all the inhabitants stand in awe of Him."

So powerful was the likeness of man to God that God Himself was in awe of them. How's that for value? And before they could accomplish a single thing for Him, while still fresh upon the very ground they were formed from, God breathed the greatest pronouncement of His truth over their being saying, "very good." Their worth was not in their accomplishments, but who He created them to be. He stood back viewing them in reverent awe. Imagine for a moment, God conceiving you in His mind as a product of His greatest vision, standing back and saying, "very good!" before you could do a single thing to earn those words.

Who You Are, Not What You Can Do

God has given gifts to His children to accomplish in His authority and strength what He is sending them to do. Tessa Afshar illustrates this beautifully in her moving novel *Harvest of Rubies.* She tells the story of a truth-telling conversation between Sarah, a girl utilizing her gifts to gain love, respect, and position, and her gentle uncle Nehemiah, the cupbearer to the king who shares God's truth that set her free. "Listen" in on that conversation and allow the Holy

Spirit to lead you into personal truth. Nehemiah starts off the penetrating conversation:

> "I could see that learning to read gave you a sense of accomplishment and a new attachment to your father. I believed the Lord had given you the talent for a reason. Whenever I spent time in your company, I was struck anew by how precious you are. But you could not see it."
>
> *My eyes grew round with wonder. He thought I was special?*
>
> "But you wrapped your whole soul around your work. You established yourself in court and became the queen's favored servant. But did you feel secure and happy? Did your success give you peace?"
>
> *I choose not to answer, and he pressed on.*
>
> "Do you know why not? Because you were out of step with God's design. God's design includes the use of our talents. But do you think the Lord counted them worthy because of their abilities?" he went on, ignoring my restlessness. "They hadn't even begun their work yet when He made His first pronouncement over them. He called them very good when they hadn't achieved a single thing. They hadn't proven themselves capable. He pronounced them good not because of what they had accomplished, but because of who He made them be."
>
> *I felt myself freeze as I heard those words. I had never thought of God's response to Adam and Eve in those terms. Nehemiah was right. God counted them as good already, before they had done anything worthwhile.*
>
> Nehemiah nodded his head, as though he perceived that I was finally beginning to comprehend his meaning. "This is a life of right order, Sarah. The heart that knows the Lord as the source of its beauty and value knows freedom. You have lost yourself in the gifts God gave you. Those blessings have become your master.

"When your inmost being is in step with the right order of God, you reap His rest. Your soul tastes of His peace. Instead, your inner world produced turmoil, because you lost sight of who you really were. You lived in fear. Fear that you should prove dissatisfactory. For years, I have watched you live a disordered life. You've placed your intellect, your ability to learn faster than most, your quickness of thought and understanding at the core of your life. This was never the Lord's purpose for you.

"My child, the Lord's care for you has never depended on what you achieve. You were created for His love, not to be His work mule. Your accomplishments are meant to be a response to that love; instead, you have made love a response to your accomplishments. The steadfast love of the Lord for you never ceases. Never, Sarah.

"I will always have my standing before the Lord as His child. I will always know I can go to Him and be welcomed. That is who I am. My work is a small part of me—an assignment from God. Whether He gives it or take it away, it will not change how He perceives me.

"This is what I want you to learn about yourself, Sarah."

Nehemiah's words burned in my mind: That is who I am. My work is . . . an assignment from God. I did not have the ability to rest in the Lord's opinion of me. I had built my own measures of worth and acceptability. They were false; they destroyed my peace. It dawned on me just how doggedly I served these measures. I served them with more fierce determination than I served God. I wanted the good opinion of others more than I wanted the Lord.

Who could set the heart free but God? "Lord," I cried out, in my mind. "You look at the heart. Please forgive me for serving the false masters of my soul. Help me to please only You." I thought for a moment and then emended my prayers. "Help me to want to please only You."

> *I ran out of words. Somehow, in the quiet aftermath of my prayers, I grew still in my soul. It was a healing stillness.*[3]

The character, Sarah, deals with what believers deal with nearly every day in this social media, super-success-oriented society. But as she came back to her true core value in God, there was a quiet. The truth was a sword that cut off that second head and its nattering arguments. The only voice that spoke was the quiet one that was in step with truth and peace. Her heart was no longer divided between the love of the world and the love of God. Her loyalty was settled once more upon Him.

The prophet Isaiah wrote that those who turn back to the Lord as their source of value, who give Him their whole heart, will find quiet, rest, and peace:

> This is what the Sovereign Lord, the Holy One of Israel, says: "In repentance and rest is your salvation; in quietness and trust is your strength.
>
> — Isaiah 30:15, NIV

Isaiah conveyed this same message in Isaiah 26:3 saying:

> You will keep him in perfect peace, whose mind is stayed on You,
> Because he trusts in You.
>
> — Isaiah 26:3, NIV

In both verses, the words for "perfect" and "peace" are Hebrew for *shalowm* (*Strong's* H7965) which means, "happy, friendly, well, healthy, prosperous, favor, rest, safety, well and great." It conveys the message of "double peace," lacking nothing in wellness and happiness." It is God who keeps and guards His people as their minds are stayed, fixed, steadfast, and leaning hard on Him, because they trust Him. This word trust is the Hebrew word *batach* (*Strong's* H982) means to "confide, and take refuge, be confident and sure in." Basically, Isaiah's words mean that God keeps His people in a state of happy and complete

[3] Afshar, Tessa. *Harvest of Rubies*. Chicago: Moody Publishers, 2012.

blessing and peace as their minds are tattooed on Him—for they trust and take refuge in Him. Are you ready to tattoo your mind on Him? He'd be thrilled!

Will That Satisfy You?

A heart devoted to another source will begin to lose its "double peace" and its trust in God alone. I remember once, while doing some work in our home, I was imagining my greatest dreams coming to pass. I sensed the Lord's presence as He came and whispered to me, "Will that satisfy you?" I paused. I imagined myself in the moment as if all I had been praying and working toward happened. I checked my heart in the company of the Holy Spirit to see if this would truly satisfy me. My soul answered the question with clarity, and I spoke to the Lord "No, Lord. You are the one who satisfies me. When You touch my life, I am still, calm and full. This dream is only the outflow of us and the joy of knowing You and sharing You." I knew that this pleased the Lord.

As you become free from valuing your accomplishments, your "prides of life" above the love of God, you will be free to serve in a new and powerful way. Your motives will be tempted at times, but no temptation has overtaken such as is common to man—and God will provide a wonderful way of escape if you only ask (1 Cor. 10:13). Then the joy of doing whatever you do, secular or ministry, will be for God. But God wants your service to overflow from loving Him back and sharing that same love with the world.

Performance should not be a driving force, but obedient service with love and devotion. Performance for the love of the world and the pride of life is a fickle mistress. She will reward you one moment and turn on you the next if you cannot meet her demands. It's time to end the tug-of-war for your worth. You can serve the task master of the world, Satan, or a servant King who was pleased to make you a part of His kingdom. It is better to trust in the steadfast love of the Lord and learn to rest in His view of you.

The Canoe Dream

One morning I had a strong dream from the Lord. In my dream, I was resting on my back in a canoe with my arms folded comfortably beneath my head.

There were no oars or paddles. The lake was completely peaceful and shimmered like glass as the sun shone down on it. There were no waves, no wind; it was completely still. As I lay on my back, I thanked the Lord for the glorious blue sky above me and relished in it. I was totally at peace, enjoying and delighting in rest and the surroundings. I saw Jesus walking on the water near my canoe. He swooshed His arms forward and suddenly a gust of wind propelled the canoe forward. The canoe eventually slowed to a stop, but I was still not at the shore. I thought to myself, "Jesus is going to have to swoosh His arms again." With that, Jesus did swoosh His arms again. And again, a gust of wind moved the canoe forward—this time to the shore. He gave me a hug, but then I was on my own. He walked away upon the water to others that were on the lake. I saw Him and said, "That man has authority." It was like I was seeing His authority at one percent of what it is, but it was still powerful.

This dream is significant for the whole body of Christ. There were no oars so I could apply no human effort. I was in total peace enjoying God and His creation, praising and thanking Him. It was Jesus who supplied His ability to get me to where He wanted me to go and when He wanted me to go there. He has all authority to make those decisions. Jesus declared this to His disciples, just before leaving earth:

> Jesus came and told his disciples, "I have been given all authority in heaven and on earth. Therefore, go and make disciples of all the nations, baptizing them in the name of the Father and the Son and the Holy Spirit. Teach these new disciples to obey all the commands I have given you. And be sure of this: I am with you always, even to the end of the age."
>
> — Matthew 28:18–20, NLT

You may not be called to preach, but God has the authority to send you wherever He is calling you. Rest in His authority. He will get you to the other side. It is Jesus Christ who releases the wind and power of His Spirit to propel you forward. Even if you are called to take steps of faith, you can do so resting, praising, and thanking while enjoying where you are until He is ready for you.

The Eternal Artesian Spring

An artesian spring or well is water under the earth's surface under tremendous pressure. It springs up all on its own. No pumps or human effort are needed; the pressure helps the water spring up to the surface where it can be easily accessed by people or animals. It is cleaner than running rivers because as the water passes through hard layers of porous rock, it becomes purified. The pressure helps keep the water contaminant free.

Man-made wells can breed disease, have cracks, and leak, and be vulnerable to contaminants. They can also become clogged.

Jesus died to release His Spirit so we could be one with the Father and do greater works. By sending His Spirit, He fully intended for His people to have rivers of living water flow out of their being with force, purity, and life-giving refreshment to the world, especially under the pressure of impossible situations. That is where miracles happen.

Jesus died to give this never-ending spring of life. Imagine Him watching His children dig their own measly well. How painful that must be for Him to watch His people sinfully spurn His needed gift! This grieves the heart of God, who said through Jeremiah:

> My people have committed two sins: They have forsaken me, the spring of living water, and have dug their own cisterns, broken cisterns that cannot hold water.
>
> — Jeremiah 2:13, NIV

How much more pleasing it must be for Him when His children call on the Holy Spirit to release His life, love, and power. He is bidding you not to forsake Him and harden your heart in preference to your own strength.

Ponder for a moment the Holy Spirit, perfect in love and fully bestowed upon Jesus without measure. Together, they agreed to the plan to demonstrate the

Father. They were one and fully attached to one another in love. Together, they endured the cross, the Holy Spirit supplying the strength for Jesus to go through it. It not only pained Jesus to give up the Holy Spirit and be separated from Him at His death, but it pained the Holy Spirit to leave Him. The Holy Spirit, being omniscient, knew this death would result in departing from Jesus whom He loved completely. The Holy Spirit, of pure love, would have felt the loss of Christ with great grief. But He and Jesus were looking ahead to the generous outpouring of the Holy Spirit to you. Now, instead of being one with Jesus alone, He is also one with you:

> He who is joined to the Lord becomes one spirit with Him.
>
> — 1 Corinthians 6:17, ESV

This gift is free for you to receive but it cost the Holy Spirit and Jesus everything to give it. With a bowed and humble heart, receive the power from Him to be His witness on the earth. Do not grieve the One who loves you by forsaking the preciousness of this gift and reverting to your own strength. Treasure His gift and humbly allow the flow of the Holy Spirit to demonstrate the Father through you.

It's time to turn from being divided between personal, worldly values and loyalty to God. God has an assignment for you that can only be accomplished through His might and power.

Reflect with the Holy Spirit

Thank God that He has provided a way out of this tug-of-war. Thank Him for the truth that sets you free, and invite Him to teach you what that looks like for your life. Use the following questions to consider other ways God may be calling you to trust His authority and strength:

1. What have I believed about status or achievements before reading this chapter? What do I believe now? ______________________________

   ____

2. How does it make You feel when I relax into Your pronouncement over me of who I really am — "very good"? ______________________

____

____

3. Is there anything I believe that is out of step with Your design? ______

____

____

4. Would You like to touch any hurt in my heart that has driven me to believe I was deficient as I was? I welcome Your thoughts into that area of my life and make my heart whole and devoted to only You. What are those thoughts? ______________________________

____

____

5. Am I doubting the authority you have delegated to me and thus the power you have given me to accomplish what you have asked me to do? ____

____

____

6. How am I feeling about believing You now? Are any areas getting quieter and more steadfast as I believe? Is there less pulling on me and tempting me away? ____________________________________

____

____

CHAPTER 5 – FEAR MAN . . . OR GOD?

The eyes of the Lord search the whole earth in order to strengthen those whose hearts are fully committed to Him.
— 2 Chronicles 16:9, NLT

When I was about eight or ten years old, my big brother, Mica, was in baseball and we regularly attended his games and practices in the spring. There were often fantastic playgrounds at the fields. I had found a kid my age who was also at all the games and practices and we played together regularly. I valued our comradery and time together.

I was a people-person even from a young age. This "friend" would often say, "If you don't play with me here or there, I won't be your friend." So, I would do whatever that friend said. One day, practice was held near a school yard with maypoles. Maypoles were my absolute favorite and I was born to play on them. Who wouldn't enjoy spinning around and around a pole, feet sailing through the air and a death grip on the round metal handles? But once I was threatened with the words, "If you play on those maypoles, I won't be your friend." I paused for a millisecond, turned around and said, "Okay!" and walked off to my maypoles. I wanted to turn my head to see if this friend was following, but instead I turned my soul to cold steel and refused to look back.

I felt strong and powerful. I had conquered what had been holding me back from being my authentic self and doing what I loved. I will never forget that tremendous victory. Whatever a person's age, sometimes it's necessary to grit one's teeth and go to the maypoles . . . or in this case, to fulfill one's calling without fearing the opinions of man. God will strengthen those whose hearts are fully committed to Him as mentioned in the above verse.

Your heart and loyalty are God's greatest concern because out of it flows the wellspring of life (Prov. 4:23). Jesus is the Tree of Life, and He wants nothing but life for those who believe in Him. He knows the fear of man is one of the most common issues that can prevent you from fulfilling your destiny and will divide your heart and thus divide your faith. This is another way double-mindedness leads to confusion, fear, and an inability to follow through with God-given dreams and assignments—even though He has already mapped out each person's victory.

When asked what the greatest commandment of all was, Jesus replied:

> Love the Lord your God with all your heart and with all your soul and with all your strength and with all your mind and love your neighbor as yourself.
>
> — Luke 10:27, NIV

Jesus is on a different level than, say, a neighbor. Jesus placed Himself above any person as the Supreme God of the universe. Loving God with "all" your heart means loving Him with an entirety. No sharing. No "as yourself" comparisons, or as much as a person loves a pastor, spouse, or success. Obeying Jesus' words in Luke 10:27 is a vow of consecration and separation unto the Lord.

View this commandment within the context of your current placement of man in your life. If you had to choose who to obey, man or God, what would it look like? Would there be all kinds of arguments within you? Perhaps the natter sounds like, "I feel like God is leading me to do . . . But what if so-and-so doesn't like it? What if they don't agree? What does so-and-so think? I'm afraid I'll have a conflict if I . . ." If God is leading, obey His promptings. It will come with peace, and God is asking you to "let the peace that comes from Christ rule in your hearts," (Col. 3:15 NLT), not the fear of man.

The word "peace" is the Greek *eirene* (*Strong's* G1515), which means "one, quietness, rest, set at one again." The peace that comes from choosing to obey the Lord brings single-mindedness again—no nattering heads, only one peaceful head: Christ, who is the head of the church.

The word "rule" in Colossians 3:15 is one of the most powerful words a Christian can learn for decision making and for possessing an undivided heart. It is the Greek word *brabeuo* (*Strong's* G1018) and it means "to govern like an umpire." In other words, peace should be the "umpire" of a person's heart. If you have peace over a decision, and the decision lines up with Scripture, let it be like an umpire saying, "Safe!" Allow that peace to bring you a place of wholeheartedness again, no longer divided and tossed to and fro. If you have peace but want to be sure, ask the Lord to confirm it to you. He knows you better than you know yourself and will speak in a way you will understand.

If you *do not* have peace about what you think God may be leading you to do, trust that as well. A lack of peace can be a strong feeling or a mild unrest. Either way, it should be viewed as a clear sign to settle down quietly before the Lord and let go of that plan for the time being—or permanently—depending on His leading.

Fear Versus Cowardice

There's a difference between being fearful and cowardly, versus a loss of peace. To be "cowardly" means shrinking back due to anxiety. Fear, however, can be present with peace; it means stepping out, following, and trusting God, though afraid.

When the opinions of others prevent God's children from obeying His promptings, they are shrinking back and serving man who becomes their master instead of God. Paul highlights his personal commitment to serving God alone in his letter to the Galatians saying, "If pleasing man were my goal, I would not be Christ's servant" (Gal. 3:10 NLT).

Paul knew he could ultimately only answer one voice and revere and obey one loyalty. He chose God. God allowed Paul's life to be an example of what obedience in the face of fear looks like. He faced tremendous physical persecution by both the Jewish religious community and the gentile community. Paul was also the first disciple/apostle who had not physically walked with Jesus like the other disciples; he had to trust and obey regardless of human authority:

> This letter is from Paul, an apostle. I was not appointed by any group of people or any human authority, but by Jesus Christ himself and by God the father, who raised Jesus from the dead.
>
> — Galatians 1:1, NLT

Paul knew exactly who he was and what he was called to do, and he obeyed God despite his altogether different start than the other disciples who had spent three years with Jesus. He could have compared himself to the other apostles, but Paul put himself aside and made obedience to God his highest priority. With an undivided heart, he accepted who he was—a Christ-ordained apostle—and fully lived out that assignment:

> But by the grace of God I am what I am, and His grace toward me was not in vain. On the contrary, I worked harder than any of them, though it was not I, but the grace of God that is with me.
>
> — 1 Corinthians 15:10, ESV

The reality is everyone both fears and trusts in people to a degree, and it is something we all, as followers of Jesus, must overcome. It's easy to perceive others as having far more power; it is a fear that others will block our plans, hopes, dreams or worse—needs. It is a fear that they have power to take away our affirmation, respect, or opportunities. But God is Lord over these things, not man.

Solomon wisely described the fear of man in a word picture highlighting the pain it can cause, saying:

> The fear of man will prove to be a snare, but whoever trusts in the Lord is kept safe.
>
> — Proverbs 29:25, NIV

The Hebrew word "snare" in Proverbs 29:25 is *mowqesh* (*Strong's* H4170) which means, "a noose for catching animals, a hook for the nose, to be ensnared or trapped." This word picture is of one who walks through life in fear of man, and the potential impact man can have on his or her life. This kind of person becomes trapped, caged, hooked in the nose, and led about by that fear or person.

However, the Lord promises something quite different to those who place their trust in Him. "Trust" in that same verse is the Hebrew word *batach* (*Strong's* H982). *Batach* means, "to run for refuge for protection, be confident, sure, bold, careless."

Finally, the word "safe" in Hebrew is *sagab* (*Strong's* H7682) meaning, "to be exalted and lifted-up, inaccessible, safe, strong, and to be too strong." Picture an older brother holding an object high and inaccessible above his sister's head and the sister cannot snatch it out of her brother's too strong and exalted hand. This is the meaning of *sagab*.

Inserting these definitions into the verse brings deeper understanding to what Solomon was communicating: "The fear and anxiety due to man is like a snare that traps you and puts a hook in your nose and drags you painfully through life, but those who trust in the Lord are confident, without care, and are held up high and inaccessible in God's exalted hand, which is too strong for their enemies."

Freedom to Serve God and Grow

Consider what God said after creating Adam and Eve:

> God blessed them; and God said to them, be fruitful and multiply, and fill the earth, and subdue it; and rule over the fish of the sea and over the birds of the sky and over every living thing that moves on the earth.
>
> — Genesis 1:28, NASB

Jesus echoed this concept of multiplying people in His image. Just before ascending into heaven, Jesus told His disciples:

> Go therefore and make disciples of all the nations, baptizing them in the name of the Father and the Son and the Holy Spirit, teaching them to observe all that I commanded you; and lo, I am with you always, even to the end of the age.
>
> — Matthew 28:19–20, NASB

Earlier in His ministry Jesus had told His disciples a parable, saying:

> A nobleman was called away to a distant empire to be crowned king and then return. Before he left, he called together ten of his servants and divided among them ten pounds of silver, saying, "Invest this for me while I am gone."
>
> — Luke 19:12–13, NLT

Just as with Adam and Eve, Jesus told His disciples their purpose was to multiply believers. In yet another illustration, Jesus conveyed His message again:

> The Kingdom of Heaven is like the yeast a woman used in making bread. Even though she put only a little yeast in three measures of flour, it permeated every part of the dough.
>
> — Matthew 13:33, NLT

These are verses that not only release you to expand His kingdom, but also to overtake and conquer. He, without controlling you, releases you to discover how you can be fruitful and prosper, to invest and make disciples. That is freedom to be creative and powerful. Fear of man will shut believers down, but obedience and fear of the Lord will bring prosperity.

Fearing God Brings Peace

Fearing God brings peace and empowers the follower of Jesus to lead forth under the promptings of God and take dominion. Loving and devoted reverence enables them to hear God's voice, heed His commands, and remain loyal to Him first in their life. He will not share a person's loyalty with anyone else.

Honoring God first and loving Him with a whole, undivided heart leads to faith that is not divided. When faith is not divided, the child of God can stand firm. Often this means giving up what the person has been trusting in man for or hoping man would provide or fulfill.

I remember a time when God asked me to step out and begin to preach. I knew there would people who would not agree. I deeply wanted their affirmation in my life, and I believed that if they endorsed me, it was as powerful as if God had recommended me. I was not afraid whatsoever to be in ministry, but I was afraid of *others* in ministry who did not approve of me due to their beliefs about "covering". I feared their opinions above God's. I feared their way of doing things above the promptings of the Holy Spirit and above following God in obedience.

God knew this and was about to expose my idol. First, however, He showed me I first needed to see that an idol existed. The closer I came to obeying God, the more double-minded, confused, and unable to make decisions I became. Daily it grew worse. It became so bad, I cried out to God in desperation and asked, "What is wrong? Why am I struggling so much? What is the source of it?" I was fully prepared to receive and accept what was wrong. Anything would be better than the internal conflict warring in my soul. I did not have to wait long. In the morning as I was having my quiet time with the Lord, a verse struck me, and I knew Jesus had spoken:

> A true circumcision is not merely obeying the letter of the law; rather it is a change of heart produced by God's Spirit. And a person with a changed heart seeks praise from God, not from people.
>
> — Romans 2:29, NLT

Jesus had put His perfect and holy finger on my idol. He waited for my astonishment to pass. I was horrified and delighted—horrified because I wanted and deeply feared the praise of man and put it on the same plane as God's. On the other hand, I was delighted that He told me what was wrong. I knew He was totally and completely right. Now we could fix it together, though it would not be an easy journey.

I had revered and loved man and trusted man to make decisions about my future to minimize my own risk. If they made a mistake in leading me, that was fine. *But if I made a mistake in following God by faith*, I feared it would crush me because it would hurt to be wrong. I also feared being put to shame. It would hurt my pride and my hope that I could trust myself to follow Him—or rather, that I could trust Him to lead me. I was attempting to preserve my life instead of taking up my cross and following Him with fidelity.

But God would not have any of that. He knew that the fear (love) of man was an enormous idol in my life and had kept me in bondage. I could not serve man with my whole heart, nor could I serve God with my whole heart. This divided loyalty made me sway back and forth in my walk between those conflicting loyalties. I must have looked like a spiritual drunkard from heaven's perspective. But God is good and extended me incredible mercy. This division came to a halt one day at church. During prayer, a man stood up and read from Jeremiah:

> This is what the Lord says:
> "Cursed are those who put their trust in mere humans,
> who rely on human strength
> and turn their hearts away from the Lord.
> They are like stunted shrubs in the desert,
> with no hope for the future.
> They will live in the barren wilderness,
> in an uninhabited salty land.
> "But blessed are those who trust in the Lord
> and have made the Lord their hope and confidence.
> They are like trees planted along a riverbank,
> with roots that reach deep into the water.
> Such trees are not bothered by the heat
> or worried by long months of drought.

Their leaves stay green,
and they never stop producing fruit."

— Jeremiah 17:5–8, NLT

The next day I picked up a sermon by John G. Lake in which he quoted the exact same Scripture. He went on to say one of the most powerful things I have ever heard: "The impression I wish to leave you with is that a hundred-fold consecration to God takes the individual forever out of the hands of all but God! This is the real secret of the successful Christian life."[4]

A few days later I was reading Joyce Meyer's book *Beauty for Ashes*. In it she quoted the same Scripture, Jeremiah 17:5–8. Prior to this, I had never heard this Scripture. God was capturing my attention. Despite the three confirmations, I continued to wrestle. Finally, I said, "God, I know I need to do this but help me." God then impressed on my heart to turn on a podcast by YWAM.

The first words the speaker Darlene Cunningham spoke were Jeremiah 17:5–8. God had confirmed four times that I needed to place my confidence in Him alone. It was time to move forward and trust Him. There would be no divided loyalties, no adultery of the heart, no pats on the back by man, no human cheering section. The Lord wanted me to become rooted and grounded in Him. He brought about His goodness. In the first two meetings I held for ministry, I felt the presence of the Lord with me. A man was healed in his wrist and neck and two souls were saved. This was a tremendous test for me. Even though I experienced a bit of fear, I also experienced peace as I obeyed and honored God with my calling.

Fear of Man Affects Faith

The praise and honor of man can also divide a heart. Jesus told the Jewish Pharisees why they could not believe in Him; the Great Physician diagnosed the problem:

---

[4] Lake, John, G. *John G. Lake His Life His Sermons, His Boldness of Faith.* Forth Worth Kenneth Copeland Publications, 1994

> No wonder you can't believe! For you gladly honor each other, but you don't care about the honor that comes from the one who alone is God.
>
> — John 5:44, NLT

When given a clear diagnosis, a treatment plan is easy. That is why the Lord says to "love the Lord with all your heart." Sharing one's heart and loyalty with another is adultery. However, Scripture says, "If we confess our sins, he is faithful and just and will forgive us our sins and purify us from all unrighteousness" (1 John 1:9 NIV). Confessing a divided heart to God is the first step to that heart becoming one again. He unites it—like a surgeon sewing the two halves back together—and heals it.

With that wholeness of focus on God's praise in your life and seeking His pleasure over you, you will be able to believe in a way and measure you never thought possible before. Not only will you be able to believe God's words, promises, and prophetic words, you will be able to believe Him and His incredible character and unsurpassed faithfulness.

Because I have obeyed God's voice, I have personally experienced a greater sense of confidence and indescribable internal peace. People often comment on that confidence and peace, and I am frequently asked to mentor others. When followers of Jesus trust in Him, as Jeremiah says, "their leaves stay green, and they never stop producing fruit" (Jer. 17:8 NLT).

Fear and Control

A marvelous speaker once said, "You have no one to impress and nothing to prove." And he is right. Intellectually it's easy to agree with this, but living it is another story. Everyone has people in their life who block them with "no's." No's hurt. No's frustrate. The believer begins to fear the next "no," or how someone with more power can interrupt his or her life. Those people with power might say "no" by adding things like time, responsibilities, and relationships to the believer's life, forcing him or her to acquiesce. However, no one can control what others do. Sometimes, however, to gain approval, the person might modify his or her behavior and actions to appease others, albeit with an anxious heart. However, God says to "Stop trusting in mere humans, who have but a breath in their nostrils. Why hold them in esteem?" (Isa. 2:22 NIV).

Take yourself out of other people's hands and place yourself into God's hands, and peace and stability will result. Man is fickle. God is not. He is the same yesterday, today, and forever (Heb. 13:8), and is wholly reliable. He will remain steadfast in faithfulness to His children.

Rejection—Hit It with Your Best Shot

As you read this book, you may be called by God to step out and do something new. Maybe it's starting a new organization or a marketing company. Maybe it's creating a witty invention, preaching, or writing a book. Likely, someone will discourage you from taking that step and saying something like, "That's already been done," or, "Someone else does that really well already." I know because it has happened to me. However, if God put something on your heart, it needs to get done. God has approved it so man cannot reject it.

If Thomas Edison believed what other people said, the world would still be using candles and there would be no electricity—the foundation of most technology.

It is important to lay hold of that for which Christ laid hold of you (Phil. 3:12). Your job is to be fruitful and multiply what He has entrusted to you. If you are in the will of God for your life, you have His blessing. It's *nice* to have the blessing of man, but it's not necessary. God's blessing is the believer's foundation, greatest joy, and the reason for reverent thanks. Only Jesus Christ will be saying, "Well done good and faithful servant" (Matt 25:23). Live the one life you have for Jesus Christ in utter obedience under the unction and power of the Holy Spirit.

Now, I am not saying that you should not have friends that you trust. Everyone needs trustworthy friends—but the child of God's confidence must be in Him alone. This will bring tremendous freedom in the Lord to fulfill your destiny.

Reflect with the Holy Spirit

Use the prompts below to seek God's voice to discern where your heart may be divided, following and fearing man more than God. Welcome the Holy Spirit to guide your heart into wholeness. Let God speak to you right now about whose opinion you may be regarding so highly. He will reveal it to you, so that you can confess it to Him, heal, settle into His guidance, and follow His voice.

1. Lord, whose opinion am I prizing so highly that it pulls my loyalty, heart, and obedience away from You and compromises my faith? And why am I doing it? ____

   ____

   ____

2. How would You like me to trust You right now? ________________

   ____

   ____

3. Is there a practical step of faith You would like me to make? _______

   ____

   ____

4. When was the last time I "went to the maypoles?" Is there somewhere in my life I need to do this now? ______________________________

   ____

   ____

5. I dream of going to the "maypoles" in ____________________ area of my life! My heart is growing more steadfast to make the journey. I know this because ______________________________________

   ____

   ____

Chapter 6 – Faith and Forgiveness

What is important is faith expressing itself through love.
— Galatians 5:6, NLT

A woman recently attended one of my extended events where I preached the Gospel. Her faith for her community was low and she was not a happy person. I began to preach about being forgiven but also forgiving others. The Holy Spirit began to touch her deeply. She came forward for prayer and shared that she had not been in contact with her family for seven years because they had hurt her. I felt compelled to hold her in my arms and the Lord began to minister love to her pain. Tears flowed freely down her face and she went away under the presence of God. The next day, I noticed she was not in attendance despite that she had been at *all* the other sessions.

When she arrived later in the day, she had a skip in her step and her face was glowing. She smiled at me and said, "Jesus wouldn't let me come back until I forgave my brothers and sisters and reconciled with them. Sorry I am late! I needed forgiveness, but I wasn't giving it away. Wow, I feel different."

Two weeks later I received an update that her brothers and sisters started going to church and seeking Jesus. Her faith and joy are touching her community and she has fresh faith to see God move in the lives around her.

Unforgiveness can hinder belief in God and impact a person's ability to stand firm with an undivided heart and fulfill his or her destiny. But what does unforgiveness have to do with hearing God's voice, obeying Him, and being close to Him? Let's unpack this idea and see if it's possible to find some answers to these questions.

What is Unforgiveness?

Unforgiveness occurs when a person has been hurt and hasn't forgiven the person who hurt them. Sometimes when we are hurt, we can become bitter or attached to the pain and remember it regularly. Ultimately, unforgiveness is a love issue. Loving people should reflect how God loves. Paul described God's love best in his first letter to the Corinthians:

> Love is patient, love is kind . . . it keeps no record of wrongs. Love never fails.
>
> — 1 Corinthians 13:4, 5, 8, NIV

> Love bears all things, believes all things, hopes all things and endures all things.
>
> — 1 Corinthians 13:7, ESV

I remember one day when the Lord reminded me of His declaration that He is love (1 John 4:8). I began to replace the word "love" with "God" in 1 Corinthians 13 and view it over myself and others. First Corinthians 13 reveals how God feels about His people, and what that kind of love looks like. God is patient with His children, and kind. But notice what 1 Corinthians 13:5 says: Love keeps no record of wrongs. If God is love, *then He keeps no record of wrongs.* In fact, He says that He blots out our transgressions for His own sake. Forgetting is a gift He gives Himself, not just us (Is. 45:25). It allows Him to restore relationship with us as if nothing had happened.

To "keep a record of wrong" means harboring hurt against another or remembering the hurt in light of the deed. The world demands payment for sin; this is an antichrist spirit in which one person accuses another person in his or her heart and assigns a sentence or condemnation against the person. Ultimately, keeping a record of wrong divides one's heart and loyalty.

This means that to walk in step with the Lord, followers of Jesus must also keep no record of wrongs that others have committed against them, since God keeps no record of wrongs done to Him against those He loves.

Satan, on the other hand, stands before the Lord accusing the brethren day and night demanding God's punishment. Punishment is different than discipline. Discipline involves teaching, learning, and growing. Good fathers teach; God the Father is a loving teacher. Punishment, however, involves torment. It does not involve learning, but only the weight of a sentence that is inescapable.

But the love of God forgives the debt of the wrong one at His expense. Sometimes people hurt others more than they could ever repay. The same is true of God and His children. All have sinned more than they could ever repay. When part of a person's heart is loyal to demanding that the other person pay them back for hurt they have caused, he or she displays a love of the world and an antichrist spirit. However, forgiving others as Christ forgave displays loyalty to the heart of God and demonstrates His heart to the one they are forgiving. A divided heart, on the other hand, is loyal to receiving forgiveness, but disloyal to giving it away. It is loyal to demanding payment.

Does Forgiveness Affect Faith?

Jesus connected faith with forgiving others and keeping one's heart in step with His. Kenneth Hagin once said, "Faith works by love; if we are not walking in love our faith is not working." Where there is a lack of love for God, there will be a lack of faith. Consider Jesus' words in Mark 11:

> Whenever you stand praying, forgive, if you have anything against anyone, so that your Father who is in heaven will also forgive you your transgressions. But if you do not forgive, neither will your Father who is in heaven forgive your transgressions.
>
> — Mark 11:25, NASB

Jesus tied faith with forgiveness in another passage, when He instructed His disciples:

> It is inevitable that stumbling blocks come, but woe to him through whom they come! It would be better for him if a millstone were hung around his neck and he were thrown into the sea, than

> that he would cause one of these little ones to stumble. Be on your guard! If your brother sins, rebuke him; and if he repents, forgive him. And if he sins against you seven times a day, and returns to you seven times, saying, "I repent," forgive him.
> The apostles said to the Lord, "Increase our faith!" And the Lord said, "If you had faith like a mustard seed, you would say to this mulberry tree, 'Be uprooted and be planted in the sea'; and it would obey you."
>
> — Luke 17:1–6, NASB

To better understand what Jesus was teaching in this passage, it's important to first understand that He *is* love. The Ten Commandments are about love, and though they may appear restrictive—don't steal, don't covet, don't lie—they are actually protective. Stealing, coveting, and lying hurts others and may cause a person to remain in a state of unforgiveness because their heart has been wounded. If they have trouble forgiving, it affects their faith. That is when it really becomes a problem for God because faith is the basis by which a person can be in relationship with Him and hear His voice.

Jesus also taught when a brother sins against another believer, we are to rebuke the one who sinned. However, most people bear the sin quietly and try to forgive quietly. I am convinced this is where bitterness creeps in. It takes courage to confront hurt and sin, but it needs to be done. Minimizing sin says, "It's not a big deal," and thus, it minimizes the person's worth who was sinned against. When a person doesn't feel valuable, they might become bitter and resentful. To clear up this challenge, John the apostle instructed us to bring sin out into the open:

> But if we walk in the light, as he is in the light, we have fellowship with one another, and the blood of Jesus, his Son, purifies us from all sin.
>
> — 1 John 1:7, NASB

Bringing another's sin to the light also brings to the light your hurt so that the other person can see it and acknowledge it. The blood of Jesus will cleanse the other person if they repent. However, if the offending party does not repent, you have still walked in the light, acknowledged your value, and set a boundary. If *you* have sinned against another, however, repent and tell the person you are sorry. They may tell you how you hurt them, which will be uncomfortable; but they need to bring to the light their pain as well so that it doesn't evolve into unforgiveness on their end of the relationship, which could lead to additional faith issues between them and the Lord.

Doing so will make it possible for each party to dwell with Jesus in the light. Satan attacks what is hidden, but he cannot lay hold of anything in the light (John 1:5). This will re-establish relationship by putting it back on good ground.

Faith Like a Mustard Seed

When Jesus told His disciples it would be better for them if a millstone were hung about their neck than to cause one of God's little ones to stumble, His disciples asked Jesus to increase their faith (Luke 17:5). They were scared when they heard this. But Jesus responded that they needed to have faith *like* a mustard seed; then they could speak to the mulberry bush and it would be uprooted and cast into the sea.

Many texts have switched the text to read "faith as small as a mustard seed" but size has nothing to do with it. Mustard seeds are unique seeds. They can endure fire and remain fertile. They can tolerate water and not drown. They spread contagiously and rapidly, can withstand great hardship, and are unaffected by their surroundings. Consider how the Lord describes His love toward you. It looks quite a bit like the mustard seed of faith Jesus was describing to His disciples. Faith works through love:

> When you pass through the waters, I will be with you; and when you pass through the rivers, they will not sweep over you. When

> you walk through the fire, you will not be burned; the flames will not set you ablaze.
>
> — Isaiah 43:2, NIV

Love never fails. It endures all things, hopes all things, and *believes* all things. Therefore, if love is like a mustard seed, it will endure outward obstacles and remain unaffected and un-killable, as will faith. Where there is love, faith will work through those barriers—even ones that seem impenetrable. *Remember*: love forgives and keeps no record of wrongs. This does not mean taking abuse or letting a person sin against you; rather, address it as Jesus commands, but then discharge the debt.

Jesus taught His disciples that love and forgiveness beats in time with God's heart. Therefore, the child of God who loves and forgives keeps his or her heart undivided from the love of the world and releases the faith they need to see the impossible happen.

Corrie ten Boom and the Nazi Soldier

One day, Corrie was giving a talk at a church about God's love. She nearly froze, paralyzed with shock, when she saw one of her Nazi guards. He had been exceptionally cruel. She regained her composure and finished her talk. She desperately wanted to escape, but there were hands to shake and people to greet. Suddenly the man came up to her and introduced himself; she knew him all too well. With tears, he confessed his sin to her and asked her to forgive him. He said he knew Jesus had forgiven him, but he knew he must ask her as well.

Corrie cried out to the Lord. She knew she had to forgive the man, but she was in a battle. Finally, she surrendered by faith and told the Lord she would lift her hand to take his, but that God must supply the love. Miraculously, despite her suffering, when she touched his hand, the love of Jesus began to flow, and she said, "I forgive you, *brother*." She experienced so much of the love of God, but she also *obeyed* God. By bringing her heart into alignment with His, her heart's loyalty and her faith remained undivided. Corrie ten Boom was an incredibly fruitful woman, seeing thousands saved into God's kingdom.

However, few have suffered as much as she suffered. Whatever you are bearing, it is just as real and just as difficult. Today, if you will lift your hand, God will supply the love you need for miracles to again flow in your life. Resist the love of the world that demands payment and let your heart beat in time to the love of Christ, undivided in His forgiving love. Your faith will work through His love, and together with harmony and power, you will see the impossible.

Reflect with The Holy Spirit

Invite God to reveal people you need to forgive. Ask Him to repair your heart and your faith and to face the hurt you may have projected toward any individuals. Thank Him that it is His pleasure to sit with you, speak to you, and heal you as you forgive. Use the prompts below to help you think through this concept of forgiveness.

1. Lord, is there anyone I need to forgive? Show me how You want to heal my heart. Will You heal it? ______________________

   ____

   ____

2. Is there anywhere I need to "lift my hand" so to speak as Corrie ten Boom did? ______________________

   ____

3. Have I demanded payment from anyone? Have I given forgiveness freely as You have? Remind me. ______________________

   ____

   ____

4. Do I need a greater appreciation of Your mercy and forgiveness to be able to fully forgive others? ______________________

   ____

   ____

5. Am I excited to have a whole heart and believe for new things when I forgive? ____
____
____

Chapter 7– Money Versus God

No one can serve two masters. Either you will hate the one and love the other, or you will be devoted to the one and despise the other. You cannot serve both God and money. — Matthew 6:24, NIV

When God first called me to ministry, I went through a time of waiting on the Lord and intense study. I sensed in my heart that my waiting period was to be three years. It was a step of faith for me and my family. In the beginning, I had shared God's leading with my husband that the Lord was calling me into full-time study. Within days, a powerful confirmation came to my husband that God had it right; I was to pursue a few years of study in preparation for my personal ministry, but also for us as a couple. Soon, I was happily immersed in Greek and Hebrew, dissecting Scriptures and coming alive as the Holy Spirit led me through the Word of God. But something else also began to happen.

I daily struggled to believe I could accomplish everything He wanted me to accomplish, or that this investment of time was worth the cost. I felt guilty for putting my family through this time and for following me on this journey; from an earthly standpoint, it meant less financial security. The enemy plagued me daily with thoughts of, "You are wasting your life. You're going to have nothing to show for this. By the way, you *need* money! Look at how successful so and so is!" I equated success with financial security—and obedience and the desire to follow Jesus wholeheartedly did not necessarily promise extra money! The mental torment was thick, as obedience to God spoke to my heart with one mouth, while my desire to be financially stable spoke to my heart with the other. I was battling double-mindedness, and it was exhausting.

God Warns Before Sin Occurs

At one point during my studies, I had a dream I was a prostitute and had walked into an apartment. My husband was with me. I said, "Hey, this will be good. I can work. I've got this all worked out. I can make some money and it will be great." My husband responded casually, "Okay, sure. We can do that," and went along with my plans. A person went into a room to prepare for the services they desired. My mind suddenly cleared, and I said, "What am I doing? This is crazy! God will provide! Let's get out of here." Again, my husband said, "Okay, sure. We can do that." We left that apartment swiftly. I woke up, puzzled by the dream, and stumbled out of bed to make my coffee, read, pray, and begin my day.

Not long into my studies that same morning, I began thinking of how I could purchase a new car for our family. I imagined a certain number of hours I could work and how much I could make per month, while continuing my studies to prepare for ministry. I came up with a great plan. My anxiety and stress about success and money had settled down somewhat, and I began to feel in control again. When my husband came home for lunch, I shared my fantastic plan with him. His response was, "Okay, sure. We can do that." We enjoyed a great lunch, and my world seemed brighter. I felt good.

However, as I drove down our street after dropping my husband back off at work, the Lord spoke clearly: "This is *that*!" as He flashed the dream through my mind. My soul was arrested before God. Deep shock and shame hit me. The Lord, whose eyes see the motives of all hearts and souls, had seen mine. He saw my heart departing from Him long before I did, before I could even act on it, and He released the warning. He knows His children's days before any of them come to be (Ps. 139:16); He warns His children of potential sin before sin occurs. My heart had departed from pure and simple devotion to Him in my studies and in preparation for ministry because I wanted to make money, feel secure, and buy a car.

I had hurt Him, and I was deeply ashamed. I was thankful for the correction, but for a few moments I felt like the man who beat his breast and said he was a sinner but would not even look up to heaven. I was not condemned, but I was deeply convicted. From the Lord's perspective, He had entrusted me with a preparation time, calling, and gifts. He was committed, but I was not . . . but I did not know it. I repented.

I immediately called my husband and shared the dream and what the Lord had said as I was driving home. I then said, "God will provide." I told him we needed to stay on track and complete God's work. The response was the same as in my dream, yet again: "Okay, sure. We can do that." We were back on track.

It was God's mercy to show me what was happening in my heart so I could repent. He gave the dream in the context of marriage and harlotry, so that I would understand the level of commitment He had to me and the level I needed to have with Him. I was reminded of the prophet Hosea's words:

> A spirit of prostitution is in their heart; they do not acknowledge the Lord.
>
> — Hosea 5:4, NIV

This is a solemn verse. This word "acknowledge" in Hebrew is *yada* (*Strong's* H3045) which means, "to observe and think about and to know by experiencing." Those who have been walking with God for some time have likely experienced His faithfulness in the past; even when they were faithless, He remained faithful because He can't deny Himself and stop being who He is. Attempting to provide on one's own what God says *He will provide* hinders a person from knowing Him by experiencing His faithfulness.

A prostitute has no commitment to anyone. She is committed to herself. This imagery contrasts marriage and faithful fidelity. Throughout Scripture, God refers to sin as adultery, harlotry, and prostitution simply because it is born out of self-interest and self-care. However, in marital commitment, the spouse remains within the confines of boundaries that allow for greater intimacy. Each spouse dedicates him or herself to the other person's happiness and needs. I had devoted myself to the Lord and to the needs of His kingdom, but cheated on Him in my heart with money, self-interest, and the status of possessing a new car. I was being double-minded and had two masters. Thankfully, the Lord was gracious to alert me, forgive me, and set me back on track.

I thought I had given God my whole heart, but He needed me to experience what that faithfulness looked like in real life. When I returned to the Lord with my whole heart, I returned with fidelity—with a commitment to my first love.

Two Horses and One Rear End!

One of my favorite movies is *Sweet Home Alabama* starring Reese Witherspoon. Reese's character, Melanie Smooter, married young. After a series of painful events, she left her childhood sweetheart (now husband) in Alabama and headed for New York. There Melanie pursued a life that she hoped would fill her hurts—and for a while, it did. She met a new man in New York who wanted to marry her. The problem was her husband in Alabama would not divorce her. He wanted her back knowing they were supposed to be together. She fought him tooth and nail and finally, he signed the papers.

But as she walked down the aisle to meet her new husband, her lawyer stopped her. She asserted, "He signed the divorce papers!" The lawyer replied, "Yes, he did. But you did not." Melanie was aghast. Subconsciously, she had two loves and as a result, forgot to sign. Her dad spoke up and said, "You can't ride two horses with one rear end, Honey!" Her father's words hit her like lightning. She had already given her heart—her whole heart—to her first husband. She ran away from the wedding to tell her first husband they were still married because she did not sign the papers.

Melanie's heart had become a war zone between two loves, two masters, and only one could be the victor. The same is true of followers of Jesus. He will not accept mixed service between Him and the love of the world. Followers of Jesus can't ride two horses with one rear end.

Two Masters

Jesus knew money would be a struggle for His followers. That is why God the Father sent Jesus to reveal His heart on the matter and warn His children that they could not serve both God and money (Matt. 6:24).

A slave is committed to the will of his master. No slave can commit his whole will to two masters; his service would be divided. There would always be one master he liked better and to whom he would be more devoted. Eventually, the slave's heart would become hostile toward one master. Moses described an example in the book of Exodus of a servant who willingly became a bondservant out of extreme love for his master. It is a picture of the type of devotion God desires:

> And if the servant shall plainly say, I love my master, my wife, and my children; I will not go out free: Then his master shall bring him to the judges; he shall also bring him to the door, or to the doorpost; and his master shall bore his ear through with an awl; and he shall serve him forever.
>
> — Exodus 21:5–6, NKJV

In ancient biblical times, when a servant voluntarily served his master, he was called a "bondservant." After approved by the judges of the land, the master would take the servant to a doorpost and put him against it. He would take an awl—a sharp, pointed object—and pierce the servant's ear with it. The pierced ear would serve as a notification to the whole world that this person was a bondservant for life because he loved his master and *chose* to be his master's slave. The slave's needs became his master's responsibility; service to his master was the slave's only responsibility.

Throughout the New Testament, the word "bondservant" or "slave" or "servant" was symbolically used to describe a person devoted to Jesus. Subsequently, that person's needs become Jesus' responsibility.

Paul declared many times that he was a bondslave of the Lord Jesus Christ. For example, Paul began his letter to the Romans saying, "Paul, a bondservant of Christ Jesus, called as an apostle, set apart for the gospel of God" (Rom. 1:1 NASB). Although Paul was a free-born Roman citizen and had a great deal of status and security as a Pharisee, he counted it as worthless so that he could lay hold of knowing the Lord Jesus and making Him known. He made his choice and stuck with it with his whole heart until the end of his life.

Fear, Money, and Godly Preparation

Sometimes people are devoted to making money out of fear. It has never been God's plan that His children walk in fear. That's why He has devoted half of Matthew 6 to calming those concerns. Jesus taught His disciples how to prioritize money in their lives by faith, and how to trust Him, not the money:

> Do not store up for yourselves treasures on earth, where moths and vermin destroy, and where thieves break in and steal. But store up for yourselves treasures in heaven, where moths and vermin do not destroy, and where thieves do not break in and steal. For where your treasure is, there your heart will be also.
> The eye is the lamp of the body. If your eyes are healthy, your whole body will be full of light. But if your eyes are unhealthy, your whole body will be full of darkness. If then the light within you is darkness, how great is that darkness!
> No one can serve two masters. Either you will hate the one and love the other, or you will be devoted to the one and despise the other. You cannot serve both God and money.
>
> — Matthew 6:19–24, NIV

Jesus was not teaching it is wrong to save money, for according to the Bible even ants know how to store up for the winter (Prov. 6:6–8; 30:25). Rather, Jesus taught His disciples to guard against treasuring up material things and making them their security. Those things are temporal, while heaven is eternal. Jesus was encouraging believers to give thought and care beyond their retirement to their *eternal retirement* by sharing what they have with those who have less; He will reward those who do. Those whose hearts treasure money will be attached to money.

He was also encouraging His followers to have single vision. If the "eye" of a person's heart is focused on one thing—the Lord—his or her whole body will be full of light. If not, they will see double, and it will be like walking in darkness; it will cause a lot of stumbling.

Think of a tight rope walker. He stays balanced with a bar, but he also keeps his eye on a single focal point in front of him. If he looked at two focal points, he would have a difficult time going straight and making it to the end without falling. Eventually one focal point will win and cause him to lose his balance and fall. That is why the Lord and His kingdom must be the believer's single focus:

> Therefore, I tell you, do not worry about your life, what you will eat or drink; or about your body, what you will wear. Is not life more than food, and the body more than clothes? Look at the birds of the air; they do not sow or reap or store away in barns, and yet your heavenly Father feeds them. Are you not much more valuable than they? Can any one of you by worrying add a single hour to your life?
>
> — Matthew 6:25–27, NIV

Parents take care of their kids. My eight-year-old does not worry if I will buy him winter boots or feed him. He pleases me, and it is my responsibility to provide those things for him. It increases his trust in me. I love that he assumes that when he rolls out of his toasty bed in the morning, there is cereal to eat, and he can fill his little belly. Yet children of God fret, thinking God doesn't care about their needs when in fact, He cares more.

God only asks that His children put His kingdom first; He longs for His children to seek Him with their whole heart and be solely devoted to Him. He will add all that they need. So, don't worry and give in to the battle of having double-vision, focusing on both money and God. God will provide.

Trust God for Provision

Corrie ten Boom travelled the whole world in God's service. She would lay out a map and ask Jesus where she was to go. He would instruct her, and she would make her plans. Many times, she had to trust that funds would be available when she was in need. Often when she was about to leave for a different country, not knowing how she would be able to board the plane she had booked, someone would provide the funds (in those days people could book a flight but pay when they were about to board). It made for some stress, but her faith grew enormously as she learned to believe and trust in God's good character to provide for all He guided her to do.

One day, God spoke to her during a prayer time that she was no longer to ask churches or any person for an offering. She was troubled by this, not knowing how the Lord would provide. Nonetheless, she trusted. That day in the mail she received a letter from a person close to her who had been praying regularly for her. This person wrote, "The Lord has shown me that you are not to ask any more for an offering but to trust the Lord." That was the confirmation that Corrie needed to be sure of the Lord's leading.

God knew it was better for her to lean only on Him with an undivided heart and not to trust in man to provide. This allowed her to fix her attention completely on service to Him and not worry if her messages were well received or not. It allowed her to travel anywhere, to any church or group of people that needed her and the Lord's messages, without thought of payment. Her heart was free to be completely devoted to Him.

A Modern-Day Repentance

There is a concerning trend taking place today even among seasoned preachers and teachers. The explosion of the Internet and social media and the subsequent surge of marketing has opened the door to greater access to finance; this has led to an increase in Bible teachers worldwide charging money to take "courses" on their teachings. These are not schools of ministry but teaching messages that God has given them by the Holy Spirit. However, when Jesus

sent out His disciples, He told them, "Freely you have received, freely give" (Matt. 10:8 NASB).
Jesus should be the believers' model and Scripture their plumb line. When Isaiah the prophet testified by the Holy Spirit about what the Messiah would do, he said:

> The Spirit of the Sovereign Lord is upon me, for the Lord has anointed me to bring good news to the poor.
>
> — Isaiah 61:1, NLT

When John sent his disciples to confirm Jesus was the messiah, Jesus declared to them:

> Go back to John and tell him what you have heard and seen- the blind see, the lame walk, the lepers are cured, the deaf hear, the dead are raised to life, and the Good news is being preached to the poor.
>
> — Matthew 11:4–5, NLT

One aspect of messianic proof was not the miracles Jesus did, but whether He preached to the poor. Jesus never waited for people to pay a fee or a tithe at the local synagogue. He went out to the hills and spoke from boats at the edge of the shores of the Sea of Galilee so that multitudes could come—rich or poor. There is no record of Jesus charging people to hear Him speak. But there is a record of Him instructing His disciples regarding possessions:

> Carry no money belt, no bag, no shoes; and greet no one on the way. Stay in that house, eating and drinking what they give you for the laborer is worthy of his wages.
>
> — Luke 10:4, 7, NASB

His followers were to take the gospel and freely give it, trusting in God's care for their needs as they went. People donated food and shelter. Jesus even received finances from high-society women and those who had been blessed by His ministry (Luke 8:3). But He never required anyone to pay.

Jesus' mission was to represent the Father, and fathers do not charge their children for their wisdom. Recall that *your* mission is the same as His:

> As the Father sends me, I am sending you.
>
> — John 20:21, NIV

As Jesus sent them into their international ministries to teach, make disciples, and baptize, He said:

> All authority in heaven and on earth has been given to me. Therefore, go and make disciples of all nations, baptizing them in the name of the Father and of the Son and of the Holy Spirit, and teaching them to obey everything I have commanded you. And surely, I am with you always, to the very end of the age.
>
> — Matthew 28:18–20, NIV

Many of the Lord's ministers have books that God has blessed and turned into bestsellers, but they do not charge to take a "course" on the book. They simply teach the Word and upload it to the Internet or other media. Those who wish to go through the teaching in more depth or at a slower pace than a sermon can purchase the book. But the whole world has free access to what the Lord has freely given them, and they, in turn, are making disciples internationally. The body of Christ must return to Jesus' model of discipleship, and freely give what the Holy Spirit has so generously given.

I wish to point out that there are ministers that charge for a "course", but you can still find their teachings on YouTube or other media for free. It is more that the learner is paying for formatted material. They have been incredibly generous in sharing what the Lord has given them.

When our children were little, we had to pray for every jug of milk and loaf of bread. We were avid tithers and givers. God met our needs, but the last thing we could afford was a "course" on faith or trusting God. Yet, it is these people who are struggling, like we were struggling, that need to be strengthened with biblical teaching during difficult times.

Despite this age of rapidly changing technology, it is time to return to preaching the gospel to the poor. As the kingdom is put first, everything will be added by the Father (Matt. 6:33). In doing so, believers' hearts will not be divided between meeting the needs of those they are called to serve and their own needs and desires.

A Matter of Heart, Not Money

There are people God selects to work in the business world to amass wealth for the sake of the gospel or the needy. It is as much a ministry before the Lord as being a pastor or missionary. They love God and serve Him by making money for His purposes, and their hearts are devoted to Him. One such man was asked by God to give 3.5 million dollars. It was his entire profit, and it had taken a great deal of hard work to accumulate. He swallowed hard, wrote the check, and started from scratch. His heart was devoted to the kingdom and he was a servant within it; he understood that his gold and silver were God's.

A few short years later he had more than surpassed what he had given. He could truly be trusted with wealth, the heart of God, and true riches—eternal souls.

God wants your whole heart, too. When you trust, seek, or love money, it divides your heart, creates instability, and pulls at your devotion. Commit to God that you will stop cheating and "riding two horses with one rear end!" When your heart is undivided, you will be free to serve God wholeheartedly, trusting His incredible character and that He will provide and care for you.

Reflect with the Holy Spirit

Let God reveal your thoughts and beliefs about money, trust, greed, or fear. Remember that He is compassionate and there is no need to be anxious. Use the questions below to spur your mind toward God's heart on this issue, trusting that He loves you unconditionally and wants to help you become devoted to Him alone and not to any material thing.

1. Lord, if I was riding two horses with one rear end, what would those horses be? ____
____
____

2. Am I afraid regarding money, or the lack of it? Is money motivating my decisions? What are Your thoughts Lord? ____________________
____
____

3. Am I greedy at times, or do I buy too many things? ________________
____
____

4. How can I put Your kingdom first and free my heart to serve You wholeheartedly? _______________________________________
____
____

5. How is believing in Your awesome provision setting the stage for a new adventure in trusting You? ______________________________
____
____

CHAPTER 8 – A DEVOTED HEART, AN ESTABLISHED LIFE

In righteousness, you will be established. — Isaiah 54:14

Daniel Kolenda Dream

One night I had a dream I was sitting across from Daniel Kolenda, and world-renowned evangelist. His face was serious, and his eyes fiercely and firmly held mine until he knew he had my absolute and total attention and focus. As his eyes unflinchingly held mine, he authoritatively asked, "Are you a lawbreaker?" His piercing gaze and authority demanded a completely truthful response. I felt myself surrender internally to conviction. I was willing to die rather than lie or hide. I unflinchingly held his gaze in return and said, "Yes, I am a lawbreaker." Then I woke up.

I asked the Lord what this dream meant and puzzled for a few days. I knew that Daniel Kolenda was a man and minister of integrity, but I knew it was the Almighty I had just encountered. He took the form of someone who I would recognize as a person of great integrity and authority so that I might relate to *Him* as such within the encounter. I am very sensitive to a clean and clear conscience so lying is not something I am comfortable with. But a lawbreaker? This was not something I perceived in myself. I knew that this was a prophetic dream for the body at large.

A few more days after the dream, the Lord caused me to stumble on this verse:

> Lord, we show our trust in you by obeying your laws
>
> – Isaiah 26:8, NLT

And there it was in black and white. The revelation I wish to leave you with is this: It takes trust to obey God, the Lawgiver. It requires a ceasing from your own works and finagling to trust and obey His laws and believe that things will come out right and prosper in the end. The surrender I experienced was a willingness to die rather than live in the discomfort of a lie. God is beckoning you into a place where you will cease striving and simply trust and obey His righteous ways, look Him in the eye and begin to establish your life in truth.

In a real-world context, this means that we, as believers, do not need to cheat on our taxes because when we do what is right, God will provide. In fact, we can even tithe and offer, because we trust Him enough to obey Him and He will prosper us. It means we can tell the truth and not worry about the results; our life is in His hands. We do not need to fear man but obey God. He will prosper our way, be our defender and promoter. We do not need to satisfy our lusts of the flesh because He will give us the desires of our heart in a wholesome way and satisfy our souls. No finagling required. No mental gymnastics. Just trust and obey!

God, as a good Father, desires you to be steadfast in your faith and established. Your stability comes from building upon something sure, unchanging, and enduring. His word endures forever (1 Peter 1:25 NIV). You demonstrate your trust in God's unfailing character by following His instructions and ways outlined in His Word. Doing so will result in a lasting and solid foundation for Jesus said, "Heaven and earth may pass away, but My words will never pass away" (Matt. 24:35, NIV).

Through Isaiah, God describes how He will lay your foundation as you allow Him and His Word to be your teacher. It is not one of concrete, but of precious gems to be treasured and stones of antimony—far more beautiful than river rocks. Scripture says He will build upon that foundation with precious stones and gates of crystal. He longs for you to treasure the foundations of God—His Word—like precious jewels.

Sometimes, however, our desires are out of step with God's righteous ways and can pull our affection away from Him, creating that loyalty tug-of-war. Isaiah, like James likens this "back and forth" state to the instability of the sea being "storm tossed and afflicted." Isaiah also spoke a clear word from the Lord, that He will lay the foundation for His people that they may be established in righteousness:

> O afflicted one, storm-tossed, and not comforted,
> Behold, I will set your stones in antimony,
> And your foundations I will lay in sapphires.
> Moreover, I will make your battlements of rubies,
> And your gates of crystal,
> And your entire wall of precious stones.
> All your sons will be taught of the Lord;
> And the well-being of your sons will be great.
> In righteousness, you will be established;
> You will be far from oppression, for you will not fear;
> And from terror, for it will not come near you.
>
> — Isaiah 54:11–14, NASB

As you devote yourself completely to Jesus, with no "mistresses" vying for and dividing your heart with another desire, you will become steady and established through righteousness. No matter what storms arise that may contend for your heart's loyalty, or trials that hit that may cause you to doubt God's character, you will not be like a house that falls or a storm-tossed wave on the ocean of life's circumstances. You will be solidly established even thru trials.

In Step with God's Heart

Because God has put an understanding of what is right and wrong inside each person's heart, the human heart will never be at peace in doing what is wrong (Heb. 8:10). That is why "storm-tossed and afflicted" is such a great word picture. Have you ever seen a poorly behaved child who was happy or peaceful? The child is often miserable, crying, whining in their wayward desires. They are angry, confused, and insecure. The moment a parent has had enough of the willful behavior (unrighteousness) and, in love, intervenes, the child settles down into peace. When the child is no longer misbehaving, his or her conscience becomes clear and after adapting to being good and doing right, the child becomes happy and full of joy.

No one is happy doing wrong, even a child. Bad behavior troubles a person's heart and conscience, and often hurts those around them.

I remember when one of our sons was developing a haughty attitude. We had tried without success to train him at home, but his attitude remained the same. I grounded him from an upcoming mission trip but changed my mind because I figured it would be good for a young person to serve in missions. But when he returned home, his bad attitude showed up at work and he was fired. He was stunned and so were we.

I asked the Lord what happened, and He said, "Tyrelle, you have always prayed 'All my children shall be taught by the Lord and great shall be the peace of my children. In righteousness, they shall be established. They shall be far from oppression for they shall not fear.'" I understood immediately.

God had provided the necessary teaching, that I hadn't, to ensure long-term peace in his life. If our son learned righteousness and acted it out, he would not be in fear of losing his job in the future and would be established and secure. Thankfully, he did realize he was being unrighteous, and decided it was better to adapt to the heart and behaviors of God's kingdom and be good toward others. My son treasured the lesson and God quickly supplied a new job. Our young man has kept it for nearly three years, enjoys his co-workers, and is one of the most valued employees in the establishment.

Living in step with God's righteous commands results in peace and rest. Doing things that are wrong will produce a sense of being *out of step.* Believers must march in time to the drum beat of the Holy Spirit and the Word of God. When followers of Jesus do what they know is right, their lives will prosper and produce wonderful results. This is the joy of a well-disciplined and fruitful life. God will establish the lives of those who treasure the Lord and His ways, as He has established His own unshakeable and everlasting kingdom.

Roots of Righteousness

Our Father uses tree imagery throughout Scripture as a picture of an oasis of hope for those who long to be steadfast, immovable, and fruitful. God articulates clearly how a person can easily become this way:

> Blessed is the man who walks not in the counsel of the wicked,
> nor stands in the way of sinners, nor sits in the seat of scoffers;
> but his delight is in the law of the Lord, and on his law he meditates day and night.
> He is like a tree planted by streams of water that yields its fruit in its season,
> and its leaf does not wither. In all that he does, he prospers.
> The wicked are not so, but are like chaff that the wind drives away.
> — Psalm1:1–4, ESV

The tree is a picture of followers of Jesus who cling to His Word. Notice that it did not spring up from a little seed that just happened to fall near the stream. No, God Himself planted this tree "by streams of water." He chose both the tree and the place in which to plant it with the intention of establishing the tree and growing it to become a steadfast, enduring, and glorious tree. Streams are reflective of God, the fountain of abundant, living water. He is the source of life and enables believers to bear fruit in season and retain life so that their "leaf does not wither."

Those who *do not* delight in righteousness, but rather in wickedness, become like chaff; they are susceptible to every wind of temptation because they have no roots to hold them fast. They are here one moment and gone the next with the ever-changing wind.

The Lord used this image of a tree in Isaiah 61 to describe how He plants and establishes His children when they operate in righteousness. They will be called "oaks of righteousness, a planting of the Lord for the display of His splendor. (Isa. 61:3 NIV).

Righteousness has a steadying nature to it. To walk in righteousness means rejecting the fleeting temptations and benefits of doing wrong in exchange for the lasting benefits and peace of doing right. Oak trees are strong, enduring, and have long lifespans—often up to 600 years. Winds may blow them and cause them to bend a bit, and branches may break, but they are not likely up-rooted. When you live in righteousness, the wind of temptation can blow, but you will remain rooted, established, and flourishing as God's oak, planted to display His splendor (Isa. 61:3). You are in this process right now! Isn't that great news?

Reflect with the Holy Spirit

You are now at the end of inspecting your heart for division. You have shifted into a season of wholeheartedness. Your *whole* heart will now find it far easier to believe God's incredible character and enduring love. With an undivided heart, you will be able to live out your purpose and fight every battle with joy, knowing victory is your birthright and inheritance as a child of the living God. This will be the focus of the second half of the book. Spend some time reflecting with God on how far you have come and the new stability and confidence you are developing to fulfill His purpose for your life.

1. Lord, show me how You think and feel about establishing me in righteousness. ____
   ____
   ____

2. What does it do to You as I become wholehearted? Thank Him and celebrate as He rejoices over you with singing. ____________________
   ____
   ____

3. Invite Him to show you areas where there is now more peace and single-mindedness. ____
   ____
   ____

4. Where is my faith at this point? God doesn't change but my faith in Him does. Is it getting stronger? Am I becoming more steadfast? _____

    ____

    ____

5. What new adventures would You like me to embark on now that we have so much of these things out of the way? ____________________

    ____

    ____

6. Lord, tell me how You feel and what you think of our new faith adventures ahead? I'm listening *wholeheartedly.* ______________________

    ____

    ____

PART II – WHOLEHEARTEDLY LIVING YOUR DESTINY

The second half of this book will look at how you can put your new singleness of heart and mind into learning and accessing new levels of trust in God's unfailing love and character. You'll learn *how* to stand firm in your faith and win life's battles with your words, worship, and weapons with the expectation of victory. These tools, and others, will help you on your journey to leading a powerful, peaceful, and God–inspired adventure. Now that you have dealt with your noisy and nattering "second-head", you will be free to know and believe God, take the next steps, and do great exploits. This is where the adventure begins!

Chapter 9 – Standing Firm

"Believe in the Lord your God and you will be able to stand firm."
— 2 Chronicles 20:20

We are going to keep Jehoshaphat in mind as we start the second half of our journey through this book because he believed God just as you are about to do. He was a man who was powerfully established by the Lord once he committed himself fully to God and turned from a divided loyalty. Like Jehoshaphat, you are going to serve God wholeheartedly and not only be able to believe, but also to see and be a part of great miracles. Jehoshaphat knew his God, believed His God, and as he obediently took his army into the battle, encouraged his soldiers to do the same—to "believe in the Lord your God and you will be able to stand firm."

Every day you are writing your story and you too will be leading others to believe, stand firm and be a part of great and miracles.

What You Stand on Affects Your Stability

You can have the best of intentions in remaining steadfast in the Lord, but whether you are able to stand firm or not depends on what you are standing on and its stability. Standing on a surfboard in the middle of the Pacific Ocean with waves swelling up and down will make standing firm more difficult. Conversely, standing on the Great Wall of China in a windstorm will not be a problem. What is the difference? The stability of what you are standing on. This determines your personal stability. Of course, the Great Wall of China is more reliable than a surfboard and can be trusted as a firm foundation that will not fail.

It is the same with God's character. As you stand on His character, you take on His stability. Although God has made a promise that is to be believed, it is to be believed based on His *character*.

Reinhard Bonnke, an evangelist who has led 78 million people to The Lord, says, "People will trust those they believe will not fail them." Recall the Hebrew word for "believe," *aman*, discussed in Chapter 2. *Aman* is the act of considering someone or something trustworthy. It is the act of fully trusting or believing. *Aman* is also used in Deuteronomy 7:9 where Moses described the Lord as, "the faithful (*aman*) God, which keeps His covenant and mercy." This is the same word Jehoshaphat used when commissioning his soldiers before battle: "Believe (*aman*) in the Lord your God and you will be able to stand firm." God is the "God of the amen," or the God who will always accomplish what He says He will do. The word "amen" is more than a word that means, "let it be so." It is an oath given in a covenant, which is a promise made between two parties. God's character is the collateral on the promise:

> I will worship toward Your holy temple, And praise Your name,
> For Your lovingkindness and Your truth;
> For You have magnified Your word above all Your name.
>
> — Psalm 138:2, NKJV

The New Living Translation phrases this same verse beautifully:

> I bow before your holy Temple as I worship. I praise your name for your unfailing love and faithfulness; for your promises are backed by all the honor of your name
>
> . — Psalm 138:2, NLT

This sounds like the well-known phrase, "A man is only as good as his word." God exalts His words or promises even above His name so that His name is kept pure and spotless in its' integrity. Think of someone you know whose words cannot be trusted, versus a person whose words can. It's likely easier to believe the trustworthy person, not because of what he or she promises, but because of the person's character.

The Beauty of Covenant

Stick with me here. We are going to head into some teaching so that you will know *why* you can believe God. It will be foundational to fulfilling your destiny with peacefulness of mind and be worth every moment.

You and I are in a covenant with God. It is the basis of our wonderful relationship with God the Father, Jesus, and the Holy Spirit. The word "covenant" in Hebrew is *beriyth* (*Strong's* H1285). *Beriyth* means, "to cut." Therefore, a covenant is "a cutting." Cutting covenant refers to the ancient custom of covenant-making, a way of making a contract and was commonly used in land deals. The two parties making the covenant, or the contract, would divide or cut an animal in two and walk between the bloody pieces. They would pronounce a vow/curse: "May I be torn apart like these animals if I fail to uphold my part of the covenant." This imagery is seen in Genesis 15 when God made a covenant with Abraham, who cut an animal in two pieces; in a sleep-induced dream, God alone passed through the slain animals as a "smoking firepot." This indicated the covenant was a promise by God to Abraham; God alone passed through the carcasses, for He was the Promiser. God was making a profound statement—His very life was the guarantee the promise would be kept.

Don't miss this powerful message: The Eternal God who is life and cannot die promised Abraham He would make good on His promise, and if He did not, He would be torn apart like the animals and die, ceasing to exist. God would be willing to lay down own His life to keep His word. Centuries after this covenant was made, the author of Hebrews wrote:

> When God made his promise to Abraham since there was no one greater for him to swear by, he swore by himself, saying, "I will surely bless you and give you many descendants." And so after waiting patiently, Abraham received what was promised.

> People swear by someone greater than themselves, and the oath confirms what is said and puts an end to all argument. Because God wanted to make the unchanging nature of his purpose very clear to the heirs of what was promised, he confirmed it with an oath. God did this so that, by two unchangeable things in which it is impossible for God to lie, we who have fled to take hold of the hope set before us may be greatly encouraged.
>
> — Hebrews 6:13–18, NIV

The covenant and the "amen" declared God's faithfulness and to what length He was willing to go to be faithful to Abraham. When covenant partners finished making an oath, the one speaking it would say "amen" meaning, "let it be so." The result in Genesis was that "Abraham believed God and it was counted to him as righteousness" (Gen. 15:6 NIV). "Righteousness" is an incredible word. It means "to render innocent or just." If there were a sentence and condemnation to be handed down, a righteous person would be found just and rendered innocent. Because Abraham believed God, God considered him to be righteous which cast aside any argument, objection, or doubt in Abraham, and caused him to be quiet, still, firm, certain, faithful, and believe God's trustworthiness. This gives a whole new perspective to every single promise God has ever made in His Word or to you personally!

God wanted Abraham to trust Him. When Abraham believed God, He came into and took on the same righteous standing and stability as God, taking on God's good character and righteousness. He became like a man standing on the Great Wall of China, steady and immovable, on an unshakable, firm foundation.

Your Personal Covenant with God

Now this is going to blow your mind regarding God's faithfulness. In Genesis 12:3, God told Abraham that through him all the nations would be blessed. Although God would start with Abraham to begin the nation of Israel, He would finish His work with all the nations of the earth. Israel would be a picture of what God would do with and for the whole world. He would make *all* nations precious in His sight, not just Israel.

Fast forward to Genesis 22:18: "In your seed all the nations of the earth shall be blessed, because you have obeyed My voice." This word "seed" was speaking of Jesus. All the nations of the earth would be blessed through Him if they too would believe as Abraham did, but in God's saving grace and mercy in the new covenant. Because of Jesus, it was even greater than the one He "cut" with Abraham. It was also greater than the covenant God made with Moses, when He gave His righteous law to the people at Mount Sinai knowing they could not keep it. God already had a plan; He would enter the new covenant for both parties as both a sinless man *and* God, so that no sin could ever separate man from His love and boundless blessings; man's sin was paid for with Jesus's death on the cross.

Each of the previous covenants were "copies," or "shadows" that pointed to a better covenant. Those "shadows" were meant to show how the fulfillment of the covenant would look, and how God intended to make it eternal (Heb. 9:23). The lives of animals could not truly remove sin. The life of an animal was never a sufficient substitute for a human life (Heb. 10:24), and the wages of sin was death. The blood of bulls and goats was a temporary appeasement until the final, ultimate blood covenant was made by Jesus Christ Himself—the God-man (Heb. 9:24-28). The new covenant was made in His blood (Luke 22:20).

Sadly, each person has sinned since Adam ate the fruit in the garden. All have fallen short of God's goodness and have broken God's covenant of the ten commandments given to Israel through Moses. Man—the people of Israel—took upon themselves a curse if they did not keep the law saying:

> "Cursed is anyone who does not uphold the words of this law by carrying them out." Then all the people shall say, "Amen!"
>
> — Deuteronomy 27:26, NIV

The people "amen-ed" the covenant. Now, the consequences would be upon them if they failed to keep it just as it would have been upon God if He had not kept His promise to Abraham. Unfortunately, they could not (and were never able to) keep it—no one can. It reminds me of a story of a woman who prayed and said, "Lord, I haven't lied, gossiped, swore, cheated or coveted my neighbor's new house today. But in about two minutes I'm going to get out of bed and then I'm gonna need some help." Yes, and God foresaw that need for help well in advance and had a plan, fulfilling what no person could. To be right with God, an adequate payment for sin was needed. Jesus had to pay for, and amen, every covenant man has broken as a sinless man; He paid with His blood and death, while fulfilling the covenant Himself for everyone else.

Now pay attention to this little gem: If the wages of sin is death and Jesus Himself never sinned, then is it any wonder death could not keep Him? He was raised by the power of the Holy Spirit and resurrected from the dead. Since Jesus paid for humanity's sin and the sentence should have been death, but that sentence has already been paid, then no sentence can be given. Those who believe in Jesus receive eternal life; death has no power.

In the ultimate act of love for the world God gave His only Son, Jesus, that whosoever believes in Him will not perish but have eternal life (John 3:16). By believing and *amen*-ing God's character and covenant fulfilled for those He loves, followers of Jesus—like Abraham—receive the same reward, counted to them as righteousness. They look at the covenant God made, observe Him taking the oath and its' harm to Himself (in the believer's stead) and say, "let it be so," thus receiving His righteousness as their reward, as well as all the promises and blessings of the covenant. This gives new meaning to the verse:

> For as many as are the promises of God, in Christ, they are [all answered] "Yes." So through Him, Jesus, we say our "Amen" to the glory of God.
>
> — 2 Corinthians 1:20, AMP

Jesus was the seed through which all the nations would be blessed. He took the curse the people spoke upon Himself as a man, by dying on a cross. Paul explained this in his letter to the Galatian church:

> Christ redeemed us from the curse of the law by becoming a curse for us—for it is written: "Cursed is everyone who is hung on a tree."
>
> — Galatians 3:13, NASB

He cut the covenant in His own body so that every promise of God could be answered "yes and amen," just as God walked through the carcasses and "yes and *amen*'ed" His promise to Abraham. Not only did Jesus keep the promise for man, He *died for man,* who should have died but didn't.

You, as a Christian, do not take on a weak foundation of trustworthiness like a surfboard, or even the more stable Great Wall of China. When you put your faith in Christ, you took on the stability of God Himself. Now, knowing all of this you can sing with Jehoshaphat, "Give thanks to the Lord, His faithful love endures forever" (2 Chron. 20:21 NLT) and shout out, "Believe in the Lord your God, and you will be able to stand firm" (2 Chron. 20:20 NLT).

Look to the great lengths God has gone to prove His trustworthiness to make promises and keep them—for Himself and those He loves. He was willing to die to make and keep every promise. Your job is simply to look at those promises and believe He will be faithful to keep them based on His character. When He promises anything or asks one of His children to act on His Word or follow His direction in faith, they can know that He has paid a great price to earn their trust and obedience.

Promises Versus the *Promiser*

God Himself walked through the slain animals, and Abraham believed God's promise and acknowledged God as the "God of the amen." He was the God who would bear the curse of death to keep His promise. It was not an impersonal relationship with a promise that Abraham trusted in, but rather a personal relationship with the *Promiser*. The promise itself was the icing on the cake. Knowing God's character and faithfulness was the greatest portion. It was also knowing His protection, blessing, mercy, love, and friendship.

If Abraham had believed the promise only, it would have created instability. But when Abraham believed the *person* who spoke the promise, he stood firm. God's character is what made the promise stand. A glove cannot pick up a cup. The glove depends on the hand to give it the power and strength to keep the cup from falling to the ground. God's character is the power and strength needed to keep the promises and words He speaks from falling to the ground.

When you look at God's promises and not at Him, you will continue to look about and wonder why your circumstances do not line up with what He has said. You will constantly measure your present reality against what God promised and wonder why He is not being faithful—you will be like a person on surfboard.

However, God wants *you* stable, strong, and confident. Instead of focusing on the promise, look to the Author and Finisher of your faith—Jesus—and enter His rest.

He has secured every good thing and made those promises through His blood. He *amen*'ed it with His own body. Ponder that for a moment and rest with joy.

Reflect with the Holy Spirit

Ask the Lord these questions and ponder what He may be stirring in your heart. Recall His promises as you think on your new understanding of His character.

1. What have You promised me? Can I rest more now in those promises, knowing the price You have paid to keep them? How does this affect my faith and ability to stand firm? ______________________________

   ____

   ____

2. In what area of my life do I want to stand firm and have stability, peace, and rest as though I were enjoying the scenery walking on the Wall of China? Where am like a surfer on a surfboard? ____________________

____

____

3. How would You like me to apply Your Word or character to this area? Jesus, will You give me a picture of this? ________________________

____

____

4. Is there anything else You want to say to me about this chapter? _____

____

____

CHAPTER 10 – KNOW WHOM YOU BELIEVE

I know whom I have believed. — 2 Timothy 1:12, NKJV

Many people strive to believe God and have enough faith. They want to do everything well—even perfectly—so they can please God. However, they often find themselves worn out, discouraged, frustrated, and sometimes wounded trying to please what can seem to be an unpleasable God. The enemy, Satan, is ready to tell them they are not doing enough. They miss celebrating joys and victories because they do not understand God and His love. They don't *know* Him, and because they have a misunderstanding of who He is, they will wear out spiritually trying to please Him. By *knowing Him*, you can come into a wonderful rest and fulfill your destiny.

The Pleasure of God Versus the Love of God

It was morning and I was laying on my bed feeling quite unsuccessful. I wanted God to speak to my insecurity and make me feel better, so I invited Him to my pity party for two. I cried out, "Lord, show me how I please you." He answered, matter of factly:

"No."

"No?" I questioned. I could sense God distancing Himself, like a parent refusing to engage their child's drama.

"No," He said again.

He whispered clearly but firmly to my heart: *If I told you every time you were pleasing me or not, you would be up or down and striving every day to gratify Me. My love for you is consistent, steady, and unchanging, despite your decisions. This is the foundation upon which I wish My people to build their lives. Your love for your children does not go up or down. It is consistent and never changes. Your pleasure may shift momentarily with their behavior, but your love remains and endures through those moments...But My love endures forever.*

I understood. God loves me and takes pleasure in me, but I did not need to focus my life on shifting pleasure. His love alone is the steadying force of my life—and it is the steadying force in your life, too. God wants you to be able to say, like Paul, "I *know* whom I have believed" (2 Timothy 1:12 NKJV, emphasis added).

The reality is God is not that hard to please and He wants you to know this truth inside and out. It is hard to be steady, strong, bold, and at peace if the one you are in relationship with is up and down like a wave on the ocean. It can make you feel like you are walking on eggshells. But you do not have to worry about that with God. Learning about and understanding God's desire to be merciful, compassionate, and forgiving when you are less than perfect will stabilize your ability to believe; you will thus fulfill your God-given assignments in a peaceful and restful way.

God's Eternal Character

Even people in the Bible struggled with trying to please God. Moses, for example, longed to know whether he had found favor in God's sight. He asked God to teach him His ways so that he could understand and know God more and continue to enjoy His favor. But God wanted Moses to *know Him intimately,* not just work to please Him, and agreed to show Moses His glory—the weighty fullness of His presence. God was pleased to show Moses Himself—His character—telling Moses, "I will make all my goodness pass before you, and I will call out my name, Yahweh, before you. I will show mercy to anyone I choose and I will show compassion to anyone I choose" (Ex. 33:14 NLT).

God's goodness was the basis on which He wanted Moses and Israel to relate to Him. God wanted to be sure that as Moses *experienced* God's goodness, he would act on it in prayer and spread the revelation like wildfire to the whole nation. He wanted to be sure that Moses knew He is abundant when a request comes in and He does not do things by halves. When He says "yes," it's a complete "yes."

Not only did God allow *all* His goodness to pass before Moses, but He also declared His name, or His identity as a person. Consider one of the most beautiful passages in all of Scripture—when God proclaimed His very nature:

> Then the LORD came down in a cloud and stood there with him; and he called out his own name, Yahweh.
> The LORD passed in front of Moses, calling out, "Yahweh! The LORD! The God of compassion and mercy! I am slow to anger and filled with unfailing love and faithfulness. I lavish unfailing love to a thousand generations. I forgive iniquity, rebellion, and sin. But I do not excuse the guilty."
>
> — Exodus 34:5–7, NLT

God wanted Moses to know He does not just extend compassion and mercy, but He *is* the absolute source and life-flow of those attributes. He *is* compassion and mercy. He is forgiving and fair.

God described Himself again in the book of Jeremiah, so that His people would boast not only about knowing Him and understanding He is the Lord, but also that His rule, reign, and actions flow from His beautiful character of unfailing love, justice, and righteousness:

> This is what the LORD says: "Don't let the wise boast in their wisdom, or the powerful boast in their power, or the rich boast in their riches. But those who wish to boast should boast in this alone: that they truly know me and understand that I am the LORD who demonstrates unfailing love and who brings justice and

> righteousness to the earth and that I delight in these things. I, the LORD, have spoken!"
>
> — Jeremiah 9:23–24, NLT

Again, God declared Himself compassionate and merciful, and One who demonstrates unfailing love. Because He created man in His image, He created His people to represent this unfailing love to the world.

God revealed to both Moses and Jeremiah His goodness which included faithfulness that goes on forever. God Himself said He lavishes His love to "a thousand generations." He was providing a picture of perpetual, faithful love to His children that would be released forever (Ex. 34:5–7, Deut. 7:9). God is eternal and His character continues to be good long after this generation or the next are gone from the earth—and even then, He does not stop being good to those He loves. Those who trust in Jesus will have an eternity to bask in His goodness.

Moses may have had some angst approaching God, but when he saw God's compassion, mercy, love, patience, and faithfulness pass by him, he knew he—and the whole nation of Israel—could rest in the relationship. Because His character never changes; you can rest in that relationship as well and fulfill your destiny with peace.

The God of Mercy, Compassion and Faithfulness.

In the book of Exodus, God had rescued the Israelites out of Egypt in a display of His might and power, as an example of His love to the whole world. He had destroyed Pharaoh and his armies and had performed other miracles in His commitment to the Israelites. However, His heart was wounded, hurt, and angered by His people He had called to be a light to the world. But Moses knew that he, personally, was favored by the Lord and that it was time to press that to the advantage of the nation. He reminded God of this, saying:

> You have told me, "I know you by name, and I look favorably on you." If it is true that you look favorably on me, let me know your ways so I may understand you more fully and continue to enjoy

> your favor. And remember that this nation is your very own people.
> The Lord replied, "I will personally go with you, Moses, and I will give you rest—everything will be fine for you."
> Then Moses said, "If you don't personally go with us, don't make us leave this place. How will anyone know that you look favorably on me—on me and on your people—if you don't go with us? For your presence among us sets your people and me apart from all other people on the earth."
>
> — Exodus 33:12–16 NLT

Amazingly, God assured Moses that everything would be fine for him. Moses wouldn't leave God's people and wouldn't let God leave them. They were at crossroads, but God still agreed to reveal Himself. Moses would see how unfailing God's love and faithfulness was and how He forgives sin, iniquity, and rebellion. Once Moses saw God's very nature pass before him, he knew he could never let the knowledge of God's character pass him by without applying it to those who needed it: God's wayward children. He begged God to forgive the Israelites and make them His own. Moses had God on the ropes, but that is what God desired. He wanted someone to lay hold of and relate to Him in a way that understood that He wanted to forgive *in the moment of sin,* so that love could endure through every situation and forevermore.

When you believe God, and as you understand more and more of His goodness and steady love and come to know Him intimately, you will no longer be insecure. You will cease striving to please Him. It gives God pleasure to see you confident in His compassion and mercy and He is pleased with those who boldly approach His throne of grace. It means you understand Him and know what you will find there. His steadfast and unfailing love allows you to experience joy, peace, and rest as you believe Him. Like Moses, this truth should embolden you to take risks to obey His leadings and promptings in life without fear of what cannot be seen. God's forgiveness, mercy, and compassion give you permission to fulfill your calling without striving for perfection, or fearing making mistakes, or being punished. It is there, ready for you, and authorizing you to grow.

Believing God Through His Word

I don't think God ever intended His children to have faith without it being reasonable. Faith is to be anchored to something worthy of faith and commitment, and followers of Jesus are blessed that the substance of their faith is the character of God. The writer of Hebrews said, "Faith is the substance of things hoped for and the evidence of things not seen (Heb. 11:1 KJV). Let's break this verse down for greater understanding. The Greek word *elipso* (*Strong's* G1679, rooted from *elpis* (*Strong's* H1680) means, "confident trust and expectation." Faith is the Greek word *pistis* (*Strong's* G4102) which means, "assurance, belief, believe, fidelity and truth itself."

Paul taught that faith comes from hearing the Word of God (Rom. 10:17), and Luke wrote that the Word of God is a seed (Luke 8:11). When a person hears the Word of God and the Holy Spirit breathes His life on it, it is no longer just a random word, but a Spirit-filled word that has substance.

What is present inside an apple seed is a promise of an apple tree. It can grow, but it takes time and the right conditions. At first glance, only the seed is visible—not a tree. Nonetheless, there is a tree within the seed, as well as the potential for millions more trees. You know that apple seed will not produce a dandelion or a cucumber plant. You can confidently expect an apple seed to produce an apple tree that will produce apples in due time.

When you receive a word or promise from God, you receive it in seed form along with the guarantee in your spirit of what you hope for and the confident assurance of what it will become. Waiting for the "due time" can be difficult but God says, "Let us not be weary in doing well for in due time we will reap if we do not grow weary" (Gal. 6:9 KJV).

I am reminded of my son as a preschooler. He received a seed in a Styrofoam cup. At first it appeared as if nothing was happening. He couldn't see a thing because the soil was blocking the view. But a lot was happening under the soil in the unseen realm, and in due time he could finally see the little green bump pushing forth out of the dirt. This is not unlike God. When He releases a word and a believer hears it, that child of God receives the little seed with the potential of something inside it growing. It begins working right away, but not in a way they can see.

I have a friend whose daughter wanted to be a mom from the time she was a young girl. Some medical issues surfaced, and the doctors told her she would have problems conceiving without drugs, or possibly not conceive at all. I heard Jesus speak to me that she would conceive naturally, so I prayed with faith and assurance with this great promise. I did not pray long—just confidently—and sensed God's assurance in my spirit immediately that it was done. When the time was right, she became pregnant, but I learned that her placenta was in the wrong position and she would require bed rest for the rest of her pregnancy. Again, I heard Jesus speak; that was not His will. So, I prayed His will and received it with confident trust. I immediately sensed it was accomplished. The placenta miraculously shifted and the pregnancy and baby were fine. But I had to wait for the "due time" to see my little apple seed become a tree.

When someone asks me to trust them, I take a quick stock of that person's character. Is this someone who keeps their commitments and word? Is this someone who is willing to put my best interests ahead of their own? What will my trust cost me? Will I turn up broke and disappointed on a matter, or is it a good investment?

God wants His children to take Him at His Word based on His character, which is faithful, unchanging, and true. He gave everything for those He loves, it costs them nothing. Those who believe come to know God more intimately.

The Benefits of Trusting God's Word

There are beautiful benefits to trusting in God's Word. It increases faith, is effective, brings peace and joy, and produces a harvest when sown.

God's Word Increases Faith

One of the greatest benefits to trusting God's Word is that it increases your faith. God is not insulted when the fruit of His past faithfulness is inspected for credibility. God created the Bible so you could see real-life people receiving real-life answers to promises thousands of years ago, and to see prophecies that have come to pass. This attests to His Word and His character. When He makes up His mind on a matter and speaks it, He follows through.

God's Word is Effective

Another benefit is that God's Word is effective. When God speaks, He speaks as the God of all faithfulness and power. His words are life because He *is* life. They have power because He *is* power. They are faithful because He *is* faithful. They are eternal because He *is* eternal. They create because He *is* the Creator. They establish things because He *is* established and *is* the author and finisher of His people's faith. His words are seeds because He *is* a multiplier, not an "adder." When He sends a word, it is so there can be a harvest. His words do not return to Him empty, as Isaiah says:

> As the rain and snow come down from the heavens
> and stay on the ground to water the earth.
> They cause the grain to grow,
> producing seed for the farmer
> and bread for the hungry.
> It is the same with my word.
> I send it out, and it always produces fruit.
> It will accomplish all I want it to,
> and it will prosper everywhere I send it.
>
> — Isaiah 55:10–12, NLT

If God has told you He will heal your family, bring you into ministry, have you write a book, or put your kids through college, then He will do it. The point of speaking His promise to you is to send His Word out to produce what He intends to happen. The only way to get a harvest is to sow a seed!

In Romans, Paul said God "calls into being that which does not exist" (Rom. 4:17 NASB). He intends to create something new in your life that does not yet exist and does this through His Word. Every time God speaks, His words literally go out and produce exactly what He intends them to produce. They never return empty, void, and without action (Isa. 55:11). His Word is effective in changing reality to match His God-ordained will.

God's Word Brings Peace and Joy

Additionally, God's Word brings unspeakable peace and joy. When God's words come to pass in your life, there will be joy and peace. The psalmist David said that when desire comes, it is a tree of life (Prov. 13:13). I remember when God spoke to me about a house for our family. I knew He would do it. And when it happened, I was filled with joy and peace. I felt like I was eating the fruit of my prayers, faith, and confident trust. Consider Isaiah's words:

> You will live in joy and peace. The mountains and hills will burst into song, and the trees of the field will clap their hands! The events will bring great honor to the Lord's name; they will be an everlasting sign of His power and love.
>
> — Isaiah 43:12–13, NLT

Look at Isaiah 46:11 which says, "Indeed I have spoken it; I will also bring it to pass. I have purposed it; I will also do it." Don't you love the *I's*? It means God will do what He spoke—not you. So, the pressure is off, isn't it? You do not have to be faithful to accomplish God's Word—but God does. If He gives you instructions, follow. If not, settle down in faith and trust with confidence in your great and amazing God. He has a great purpose in every single area of your life and in every single season of your life. His words have a purpose behind them.

God's Word Produces

Finally, God's Word produces. Consider Jeremiah. Jeremiah was a young man and prophet of God set apart for a purpose even before he was placed in his mother's womb. God orchestrated Jeremiah's birth at a time when God knew

His beautiful people would be turning away from Him to worship other gods, breaking His heart. Jeremiah was young and scared by the task ahead of him. But God assured Him through the image of an almond branch:

> Look, Jeremiah! What do you see? And I replied, "I see a branch from an almond tree. And the Lord said, "That's right, and it means that I am watching, and I will certainly carry out all my plans."
>
> — Jeremiah 1:11–12, NLT

God was teaching Jeremiah something using a picture he could understand. The vision was a parable, a story if you will, that told of God's faithfulness. Almond trees, also called Watching Trees, were the first tree to awaken in spring. Their buds announced spring was on the way; spring never failed to follow the blossoms of the almond tree. God was letting Jeremiah know He was aware of events, heralded and announced them before they came to pass, and watched over them to see that they were performed. Interestingly, the word for "almond" is almost identical to the word for "watching" in Hebrew. God wanted Jeremiah to trust Him that He was more faithful than the almond tree that Jeremiah had seen growing up in Israel year after year, spring after spring. What He announced would go forth first, and he could "watch" the reality of it follow without fail, producing exactly what He intended. And it will do the same for you.

Learning Takes Time

Real victorious belief can be hard at times, but it may be because you are still learning to more fully understand His unfailing love and excellent character. The more you learn about His character, the more you will know *Him* like a close friend, and the easier it will be to believe. Learning takes time. Knowing how the Holy Spirit is working when God speaks His power-filled words will help you believe, even when can't see the outcome with your eyes.

Reflect with the Holy Spirit

Invite the Holy Spirit to speak to you today about what it means to know Him by understanding His character. Use the questions below to help stir your heart and mind and to initiate a conversation with God that will hopefully draw you into a more intimate relationship with Him:

1. How does Your love versus Your pleasure affect my stability, trust, and peace? Show me Your love for me versus Your pleasure. ___________

   ____

   ____

2. How does Your compassion and mercy affect my confidence? How would You like it expanded in my life? ___________________

   ____

   ____

3. Show me how You feel when I receive Your forgiveness. __________

   ____

   ____

4. What do I need to allow You to teach me regarding forgiveness and mercy? ___________________________________

   ____

5. Does understanding Your character help my faith? How does it help me believe You? How does it affect my next steps of obedience in my destiny and calling? ___________________________

   ____

   ____

6. What words or promises do I need to "watch" for? _____________

   ____

CHAPTER 11 – TRUST IN THE PROPHETS

Put your trust in the prophets and you will succeed. — 2 Chronicles 20:20

Are you ready to spend days and even seasons gathering plunder within your destiny? Then get ready to embrace the prophetic voice of God! Remember how Jehoshaphat's trust in the prophets turned Israel's battlefield into *The Valley of Blessing?* So great was God's blessing, it took three days to gather it all.

Jehoshaphat understood God's prophets were spokesmen delivering His message, in the same way a megaphone clearly conveys the message of the speaker. The word "prophet" in Hebrew is *nabiy* (Strong's H5030). It means, "inspired person or mouthpiece/spokesperson." God's Holy Spirit sovereignly moved upon certain people and inspired them to speak forth His words. Picture God picking up a person and using that person as a megaphone to convey the message He longs to speak in a way His people will understand clearly. When you trust and believe God's prophets, you are trusting and believing God who spoke through them. This will enable you to win your battles and fulfill God's plans for your life with steadfast confidence.

Those who act according to His words through the prophets will succeed because of His promises:

> God is not a man, that He should lie,
> Nor a son of man, that He should repent.
> Has He said, and will He not do?
> Or has He spoken, and will He not make it good?
>
> — Numbers 23:19, NLT

I, the Lord, speak only what is true and declare only what is right.
— Isaiah 45:19, NLT

God is not capable of lying. There is no lie in Him. He is truth and He is love. One of the most beautiful things about love is that it rejoices when the truth wins out in a person's life (1 Cor. 13:6 NLT). This happens when the believer hears God, who loves beyond comprehension, and lives out what He says whether it is directional by the Holy Spirit, or through His commandments and ways. I'm including commandments because all Scripture is written under the unction of the Holy Spirit (2 Tim. 3:16). He is good and all He says and does is for the benefit of His children. Any benefit He receives comes from His children experiencing a blessed life by following His instruction. After all, if God is all-wise, all-loving, and all-knowing, then doing things His way would be advantageous.

The picture I wish to convey is a modern-day reality seen in Reinhard Bonnke, a world-famous evangelist. Reinhard had a God-ordained plan for the nations that would be in place long after he'd gone to be with the Lord. He wanted a successor to win the souls of the world. Try as he might, he could not find one on his own. After much prayer, one day he happened to go to his resource warehouse where he met a young man with the same fire for souls that he had, Daniel Kolenda. Over the next ten years, Reinhard taught and raised the young man into a strong, powerful man of God that could bear the full weight of the ministry. Reinhard spoke words of righteousness, correction, and direction/instruction.

At times, I am sure Daniel would have had to abandon his own insights to listen, obey, and learn from his mentor. If Daniel decided not to listen and learn, it would not affect Reinhard. Reinhard was fine. But Reinhard was blessed by Daniel's learning and growth. Also, the whole world around Daniel would be blessed. Daniel Kolenda is currently leading millions to the Lord.

This is how it is with God and those who trust Him. He is fine regardless of their decisions but is blessed when they follow with trust. It is important that believers trust His character when He gives commands, correction, encouragement and instructions through His Word and through the prophets—just as Daniel put his trust in God speaking through Reinhard. Sometimes God will speak to someone directly and in turn declare God's message to others. As followers of Jesus put their trust in God's true prophets, they will succeed in whatever they face.

Four Ways Prophets Speak

God's words for His people fall into four categories: Decrees of future events, corrections or warnings, promises, and commands.

1. Decrees of Future Events

Sometimes a word from God comes directly as a decree of future events. It may be something only God can do and requires His child to simply stand firm. Other times God may require cooperative actions. But both ways require the person to believe and to trust God with fidelity.

God's Sovereign Work

In our thirties, we suffered as a couple from secondary infertility. This is when a couple has children but struggle to conceive again. We wanted a third child and began trying almost right away after our second but became frustrated after three years with no baby. A prophet from Argentina said to us, "Quantos ninos?" or, "How many children?" We answered, "Dos" which means, "two." He replied, "No. Uno mas." One more! We knew it was God speaking through this man, but that child did not arrive until eight years after the last and twelve years after the first child. We trusted that word wholeheartedly and we trusted the prophet God sent as His mouthpiece to speak it. We had no doubts. Success came eventually, and God was faithful to do what He said He would do with no help from us.

Cooperating with God's Directions

I wish my whole Christian walk was like our experience with our third child listed above. But many times, God wants His children to cooperate with His

Word. He has given biblical examples so that when He speaks, they will know they can cooperate.

Moses had to cooperate with God by walking over to Pharaoh's palace, request to speak with Pharaoh—likely with numerous security guards who remembered he had been a murderer—and declare, "Let My people go!" Then he had to pronounce judgement after judgement while facing Pharaoh's and his people's doubts. When it was finally time to leave Egypt, he had to stick out his staff over the waters at God's word to part the Red Sea. Imagine if the waters didn't part?

Sometimes God will give a leader a position of being a prophet/ mouthpiece so that He can give promises with instructions, calling the people to cooperate with God. Joshua was one such leader. God called Joshua to speak out His promises to part the Jordan River so the people could cross to the Promised Land. He had to tell the priests to put their feet into the river first before the water would part:

> It shall come about when the soles of the feet of the priests who carry the ark of the LORD, the Lord of all the earth, rest in the waters of the Jordan, the waters of the Jordan will be cut off, and the waters which are flowing down from above will stand in one heap.
>
> — Joshua 3:13, NASB

That took some heavy-duty cooperation, especially for the priests. When the Jordan River overflowed its banks at that time of the year, it was deadly.

The people of Israel also had to obey the instructions given, pack up, and prepare to cross despite what they saw as an obstacle before them. But they won a great testimony and could share it with others, declaring how they obeyed and what happened on the other side of obedience. Because they trusted in Joshua, God's mouthpiece, they succeeded.

God Speaks Directly

Sometimes God may speak directly to His prophet. During one season of our lives, we experienced great financial difficulty. We sold our home but could not afford a new one. It set us into a cycle of renting with no money for a down payment. At the end of three years, I knew that I was at the end. I'm just being honest. So, I did something radical. I prayed, "What's it going to take God? I'll pay any price."

God spoke and said "twenty-one."
I questioned Him, "twenty-one?"
He replied "Yes."

That was it. He said nothing else, but I knew exactly what He meant. Twenty-one days without food. I began fasting on juice the following day. I stood on this word knowing victory was assured. I only had to follow in obedience and trust. He was the God of breakthrough and He was my God. I also knew that the coming breakthrough would bring us a home of our own. I didn't know how to pray or what to say so I just stood firm. Towards the end of the fast, I heard the Lord say, "The Egyptians you see today, you will never see again!" (Ex. 14:13). I knew I had the victory. Through a series of miracles and favor from God, one year later we bought a house with 50 percent down. We heard His word, obeyed it, and trusted Him. He brought about a great victory. We have continued to grow financially.

2. Corrections or Warnings

Solomon, the wisest king to have ever lived, said, "faithful are the wounds of a friend" (Prov. 27:6). Although wounds hurt, some wounds bring healing, such as a doctor's scalpel cutting out a cancer. A friend might see something in you and speak a correction. You can feel the scalpel touch the mark. You are then faced with the choice of accepting it or getting offended. God is the best friend you'll ever have and He's a good Father. He is love and keeps no record of wrongs because His son Jesus paid for them. But when He does look at your wrongs, it is to correct them in love so you can live a blessed life and be a blessing to others. Good fathers teach, admonish, and correct their children.

Our sons are twenty, seventeen, and eight. We have been through a lot of parenting. As parents, we are not threatened by our kids doing wrong. We do not fly off the handle when they make mistakes because they are learning and growing. When our seventeen-year-old gets a speeding ticket, we do not become unsettled. When he gets two, we sit him down and correct him. I love it when we surprise him with our cool-as-a-cucumber expressions and calm responses. The truth is, my son's challenges do not disturb my peace. I know I am a good parent. His challenge disturbs *his* peace as I bring some discipline and hold him accountable for the consequences of his choices. Correcting him is about loving him and others he could potentially harm on the streets.

God says in Psalm 30:5, "For his anger endures but for a moment, but His favor is for life." My favor on my son will extend well beyond the shortcomings he is displaying. His character will be under development for the rest of his days. I delight in him enough to not keep a record of his wrongs, and I delight in him enough to correct him on his lack of character. I delight in my neighbors around me enough to teach him how to keep them safe and not violate their well-being. I love the culture of our family enough to uphold our family values.

A true prophet comes with a father's heart that is pure, powerful, and gentle all at the same time. When Satan comes in and attacks, he is mean and accusatory. Sometimes, he will use a friend or family member in a way that causes much pain and confusion. This truth is a sword that kills. When God the Father speaks truth, He pours out grace to repent and offers a welcoming peace when the person surrenders to the correction. It may hurt, but it does not torment. James explains this, saying:

> Wisdom that comes from above is first pure, then peaceable, gentle, and easy to be entreated, full of mercy and good fruits, without partiality, and without hypocrisy.
>
> — James 3:17–18, KJV

A little correction will help you get safely to and through your calling.

A Moment of Anger and An Eternity of Favor

God saw King David as a man after His own heart, even though David sinned grievously against God. He also sinned against Uriah, one of David's dedicated soldiers who was also devoted to God. David saw beautiful Bathsheba, Uriah's wife, while she was bathing on a rooftop. He took her for himself, impregnated her, and tried to pass off the baby as Uriah's through an elaborate scheme. It failed, so rather than tell the truth, repent, and seek mercy, David killed Uriah, married Bathsheba, and hoped nobody counted the months leading up to the baby's birth.

God went after David's heart through a prophet named Nathaniel who told David a story. The story was a graphic, emotional word picture that moved David's heart so much so that he pronounced the man in the story guilty of wrongdoing. Nathaniel pointed out that David was that very man. David's eyes were opened, and he repented.

God wanted David to be in touch with His love and compassion for Uriah, but also His anger regarding David's sin. God was obligated to correct David, to protect him, and to prevent him from sliding further into sin and harming himself and the nation he was leading. When David repented, God forgave him and did not remove His love and favor from David's life. David put his trust in the prophet and came back into a right relationship with God. There is no greater success!

A Personal Correction

I had been discipling a person for about five years. We were continually dealing with her lack of tithing, and I watched year after year as her finances were constantly under attack. She would call and we would go over the Word of God and she would think about it. She was a single mom, so finances loomed heavy.

Around this time, we received a call from a local pastor who asked us to host some people. Finances were tight so, I decided we should put our tithes into feeding these people. I justified it by saying in my heart that we were using the money for ministry. I felt a twinge from the Holy Spirit and cast it and Him to the side. After all, it was not a huge feeling of conviction. Good friends don't yell at you by the way—they talk to you quietly and calmly. But I ignored Him altogether.

That night I had a dream. In my dream my best friend called and said, "God is angry with you." I woke up wondering why God was mad. Was this for real? I asked Him why, but I did not receive an answer. I knew my best friend represented someone faithful enough to wound me when I am wrong. The person we were discipling called later and asked me to pray for her because she had just tithed for the first time and was terrified that she could not pay her bills. Bam! Clarity! I quickly repented and worked out how I could properly pay my tithes back to the Lord.

God wanted to warn, correct, and teach me and my husband—not just for our sakes, but for others. He is a good Father and has the best in mind for everyone. I needed to act in faith when corrected because I believed God and His good character.

Recall that the definition of believe, *aman*, is to be firm, fixed, free from internal objections, endure hardship and faithfulness, with fidelity. Receiving correction means accepting it without objecting or making excuses, knowing God is right. He doesn't show His children their wrong unless He is prepared to invest His power and grace to overcome it. His correction houses within it the capacity to change and grow.

Warning for a Nation

Unrepented sin can cause God to become more and more serious with those He loves, just as a good parent would with a child. Parents often announce their child's consequences in advance as a warning, out of great mercy and compassion. Parents would rather their children learn from them through words and commands than through serious consequences. This is true of God as well. And just as parents delight to turn away consequences from their children when they are obedient and repentant, so does God. Parents increase the external pressure until it is great enough to combat their child's internal desire to do wrong.

Sometimes God chose prophets to go to foreign nations and announce a warning or a decree of judgment. Jonah was one such prophet. God told Jonah to go to Nineveh and warn of coming judgement. Although the Lord chose Israel as a nation to demonstrate His goodness, He often extended this to other nations because He is a merciful God. Nineveh was one such place.

God spoke to Jonah saying:

> Get up and go to the great city of Nineveh. Announce my judgment against it because I have seen how wicked its people are." But Jonah got up and went in the opposite direction to get away from the Lord.
>
> — Jonah 1:2, NLT

Jonah had clear direction from God, but he dug his heels in and refused the Lord and hopped on a ship for Tarshish. God commanded the winds and waves with the stirring of His mighty power and used the very escape route Jonah had chosen against him. He sent an enormous storm that threatened the whole ship and crew. Then the pagan sailors cast lots to find out who had upset the gods and brought about the storm. Of course, it was Jonah. So, they threw him into the sea, and God sent a fish to swallow Him. He had no one to talk to except God, and nothing to look at but his own heart. He repented to His God and resumed obedience.

The fish spat him out at Nineveh where he shouted with obedient gusto, "Forty days from now Nineveh will be destroyed!" (Jonah 3:4 NIV). God had a moral obligation to bring justice and discipline. But His compassion demanded that He announce the warning and grant an opportunity for the Ninevites to turn away from their actions.

The Ninevites believed God and humbled themselves. They did not mess around with internal arguments or objections. They trusted Jonah the prophet, acted with fidelity and in faithfulness to what they believed, and God rewarded them with mercy and spared their city. The result was a powerful and massive nationwide wave of repentance to God. It was a revival. It can be difficult to issue the prophetic warnings God gives, but the result can change history. It can be difficult to receive correction through a prophet, too, but those who put their trust in the prophets will succeed.

3. Promises

Sometimes God will send you a prophet to give a promise. God loves promises. They are invitations He gives for His children to discover His great character and strengthen their stability in the relationship. In Revelation 4:11 God says that He created you for His pleasure. When you love someone, you want that person to trust you. You likely contribute to their life in meaningful and powerful ways. You want to reach into your storehouses of blessings, abilities, and emotions and bless the other person. God always intended to contribute everything in His storehouses to His relationship with you.

His promises are His invitation to you to discover and explore those storehouses, His character, and His pleasure in you.

God's Promise to David

David loved God. He wanted everyone to be able to come to God. He knew that people were the passion of God's heart. So, He wanted to build a temple for God so that God and His people could dwell together, satisfying His greatest desire. It was also to be a house of prayer for all nations. God sent Nathaniel to tell David that he could not build the temple. But David's desire so pleased the Lord that He sent the prophet Nathaniel to tell him God would be the one to build David's house and establish it forever:

> But that night the word of God came to Nathan, saying:
> Go and tell my servant, David, "This is what the Lord says: You are not the one to build me a house to dwell in."
> "I declare to you that the Lord will build a house for you: When your days are over and you go to be with your ancestors, I will raise up your offspring to succeed you, one of your own sons, and I will establish his kingdom. He is the one who will build a house

> for me, and I will establish his throne forever. I will be his father, and he will be my son. I will never take my love away from him, as I took it away from your predecessor. I will set him over my house and my kingdom forever; his throne will be established forever." Nathan reported to David all the words of this entire revelation.
>
> — 1 Chronicles 17:3, 4, 1014, NIV

David understood God's faithfulness, evidenced in his reply:

> For you are God, O Lord. And you have promised these good things to your servant. And now, it has pleased you to bless the house of your servant, so that it will continue forever before you. For when you grant a blessing, O Lord, it is an eternal blessing!
>
> — 1 Chronicles 17:26–27, NLT

Look at 1 Chronicles 17:26–27 again. *It has pleased you to bless the house of your servant.* God delighted to promise David this blessing. God would contribute His strength and might to protect David's lineage and contribute heavenly blessing upon it. But most importantly, it was an eternal blessing. He knew that what God spoke He would not revoke. Even after his sin with Bathsheba and taking a census that displeased God, he did not have concern for losing his kingdom.

So faithful was God that he brought Jesus through David's line and created an eternal kingdom from which all people could live under His reign for all eternity. Talk about an eternal blessing and promise! What has God promised you?

4. **Commands**

One time we were fixing the basement bathroom for the boys. We had never laid tile before, so we asked lots of questions when we purchased our supplies. The store staff recommended a glue for the walls but mortar for the floor and the ceiling. Whenever we told people of our plans they would say "Make sure you use mortar on the floor." We thought it was interesting that so many people would say that, but it didn't carry much weight with us. The truth is, I think we didn't let the words carry weight. We used tile glue for the tiles on the walls.

We were thrilled with how the walls turned out, so we decided to reject the advice of others and glue the tiles to the floor instead of mortaring them. Then the glue dried and we were ready to grout. We stepped on the tiles and the worst sound pierced the air. "Snap, crack. Pause. Crack, Crack, Snap!" Every step sounded like popcorn popping as the tiles broke under our weight. We wanted to float out of there and save what tile was left. We ended up ripping out the tiles and laying new ones . . . on mortar.

Right away, I realized something. I now say it all the time: "Just follow the instructions." Good people give advice because they want you to avoid pain. They offer wisdom based on their knowledge and experience to save you heartache (and sometimes money) and to help you. But God is far greater than just good. He is excellent and pure of character. So, he sends His prophets to write out the instructions for His children to have a good life.

The whole Bible was written by prophets—people who were inspired to speak God's ways. It is important for God's people to understand they need to view each command as given by a mouthpiece, and that each word is as reliable as a prophetic utterance by God given for His children. This is one of the least talked about aspects of the gospel in first-world countries. These countries tend to talk about the love of God, but neglect to realize that the commands of God are in place out of love to guarantee a prosperous life to anyone who will do what God's Word says.

Put your trust in those prophets and succeed!

Reflect with the Holy Spirit

Invite the Holy Spirit to remind you of times past and present that He has spoken to you. Let Him bring to your mind His faithfulness and previous victories. Allow Him to fill your thoughts with promises yet-to-be fulfilled and savor the coming manifestation of it.

1. How have I heard Your voice in the past? How were You faithful? How are You being faithful now?________________________________

2. What have You been saying to me lately? ______________________

3. Recall what David said: "When you grant a blessing, it is an eternal blessing." How should I view Your promises to me through the lens of this truth?____

4. What have You promised me that I might have forgotten? __________

5. What field is my plunder in, so to speak?________________________

Caution: *Not all people who prophesy are prophets and not all prophets are to be listened to. We are commanded to test the spirits to see if they are from God (1 John 4) and to evaluate a person by their lives. A good tree cannot bear bad fruit, and a bad tree cannot bear good fruit (Matt. 7:18, NIV). This scripture teaches us not to put peoples giftings above their character and lives. Their lives will reflect their character. Take time to prayerfully consider both the prophet and the prophetic word before the Lord, considering scripture as well as the heart and character of God. God does not control, bully or call you down publicly. Rather, "...the one who prophesies speaks to men for edification and exhortation and consolation." (1 Cor. 14:3, NASB). Prophets* *with the fruit of good character and proper use of their gifting can be utilized in your life as an asset to moving forward into your God-given destiny.*

Chapter 12 – God's Word in Battle

This charge I commit to you, son Timothy, according to the prophecies previously made concerning you, that by them you may wage the good warfare.
— 1 Timothy 1:18

Two Dreams – From Storm Tossed to Victory

I had a dream that I was in a large conference center. Only a few people were in attendance, and Reinhard Bonnke was coming to preach. I wanted to sit in the front row, but my husband said, "No, I want to go to the next level." While we were finding a seat in the next level, Reinhard was leaving the venue and going up the stairs to the exit. He stopped and laid both his hands on my head and released an impartation, anointing, blessing and commissioning me forward as an evangelist. I woke up. I realized something big had *just* happened to me and something big was *about* to happen to me.

A few days later, I was invited to Nigeria, Africa by Christ for All Nations to see Reinhard Bonnke's farewell crusade. Evangelists and guests were chosen from around the world. It was an opportunity of a lifetime and I was beyond thankful to be invited. Over five hundred people from around the world were invited to attend the historic event as special guests.

A few weeks before the event, I had another dream. In the dream, I walked into a home, up the stairs and out onto the back porch. There was a barbeque going on and people milling about on the porch and in the backyard. All the way to the left of the porch, I saw a giant Wheel of Fortune game. All the tiles were blank, but I knew the answer and yelled, "It's the Margarita- The famous sailboat." An elderly lady sitting in her lawn chair near me on the porch said,

"That's right but you don't win the $10,000 prize. You guessed right but it wasn't your turn." I was easygoing and didn't mind too much.

In the dream, I went downstairs, where a Grandfather-aged man saw me and opened his arms to hug me. Love poured through my body physically even though I was asleep. I had never felt anything like that in my life. With great excitement, I looked into his face and said excitedly, "It was the Marguerita - The famous sailboat." He smiled, and said, "I wrote *all* the books, on *all* the famous sailboats." I replied, "Well, you and I definitely need to talk then." And I laughed. Then I woke up wondering what it meant. I knew, even in the dream that the sailboat represented evangelism and fishing for men but not sure about the rest.

A few days after the dream, we learned our Nigerian visa had been denied, and our passports got lost on their way back to us. God was closing the door. I was devastated, and even began to doubt if I really was called of God to preach salvation. I was storm tossed and nearly shipwrecked in my faith. Then it hit me. I had guessed right, but my timing was wrong.

I made the decision to agree with God and decree the word of the Lord on the matter that we would go at another opportunity. I stayed connected and committed to preaching the gospel in my area until God was ready to bring me into my season.

The next year, we were invited again to Nigeria. This time, there were sixteen guests and we were able to learn in depth and firsthand what we needed in order to take new steps in ministry. God had written all the books of our lives and ministries before any came to be. I had received training at the CfaN's School of Evangelism, but God was providing a field study for me so that what I saw, I would be able to reproduce.

I saw pure and simple devotion to Christ as I spoke with Winnie Wentland who had just had 8,000 rounds of bullets shot at his truck transporting crusade equipment across the nations of Africa to get to Port Harcourt, Nigeria. Each worker serves at the risk of their lives for souls. I saw thousands of trucks loaded with sand to prepare the grounds for the crusade. I saw the saved workers of CfaN envision the unsaved and the sick receiving God's love through

Christ in numbers as plentiful as the sand beneath our feet. I saw staffers relaxed with everyone and inviting them into family over our meal tables. I watched cycles of honor grow and grow between government, CfaN and workers as they outdid one another in honor. I saw the simplicity of the gospel and healing prayer unfold before me for four nights and answer some challenging questions I had for my own preaching. I watched the world-famous evangelist Daniel Kolenda's eyes fill with tears as one "mama" got healed. Numbers make up real people Jesus created and died to spend eternity with. I watched salvation happen before my eyes by the thousands. I watched as an international team assembled from all over the entire world to serve and even though they were the best at what they did, they were humble and normal. I watched as tents of people processed decision cards by the tens of thousands so that they could be forwarded to pastors and churches who had been praying for their salvation for months. Overall, I learned it took thousands of yeses by the saved to see the unsaved come to Christ.

I stood firm and worked in my calling until God was ready to fulfill His word and I spoke His word out. No doubts slipped from my lips. I spoke in harmony with the Lord while God got my field study ready. I would never have learned among five hundred guests, never sat with executive directors from around the world and had questions answered. I never would have spoken with those who risk their lives a dozen times a year to see souls won for all eternity. God is a good Father. Speak as He speaks, and the victory will come in your life too!

Perhaps you are in a place where you have received a promise from God and feel full of joy, faith, or most of all, excitement. Maybe God has made it clear to you what your calling is in ministry, business, or with your family. Perhaps He has given you a promise of a breakthrough, or blessing. Perhaps He has given you a word for your children. Either way, you have received something from God, and it is a time of brilliance. Everything inside you is full of expectation and is likely making you feel alive. Whatever you have received, that promise is prophetic if it has come from the mouth of God. God's promise to you has announced something and is full of victory and hope.

But what happens when what God promised takes a long time to come into place? What happens when everything around you seems to contradict the words He spoke regarding a situation? This is when faith in God's promises is tested.

You Are Not Alone

Most followers of Jesus will experience times of doubt and feel tossed about like waves on the ocean. They can lose their bearings and with it—the sense of hope, excitement, and even trust. But, my friend, God gave the promise because He knew what circumstances would come. Bill Johnson, the senior pastor of Bethel Church in Redding, California, said that God looks ahead into your future and releases a word that is needed to assure you He sees you on the other side in victory. He knows what you need to hear. He is faithful and He is the God of all encouragement. The promise, staked on His character, was meant to give you strength and fortitude to endure what would appear to be operating in total opposition to the promise. There will always be opposition to the will of God in people's lives. The enemy, the devil, hates it when Christians move forward with God in His will. He knows God's Word is true, but he will do everything in his power to cause God's people to fear or doubt, or to throw their hands up in defeat. Believers are in a war, and always have been . . . but those who trust Jesus are on the winning side.

In every war there are battles. Battles are mini wars within the war. Battles can be won or lost, but God has mapped out how to be victorious in *every* battle in His Word. Like Paul, it is possible for God's children to say, "Thanks be to God who gives us the victory through our Lord Jesus Christ (1 Cor. 15:57 ESV).

There is no battle that will come into your life that He did not first know about. Throughout the Bible, God has placed numerous situations to show you, as an example, what you can expect from Him and how to cooperate with Him in both the battle and the war. God is the same today, yesterday, and forever, and He is no respecter of persons (Acts 10:34). What He has done for and with others, He will do for you. As you learn how to trust and believe Him during the battles, a great stability will come into your life. You will be able to run your race with greater confidence and peace. Jesus Christ is the Lord of Heaven's Armies, and He is committed to you and His plan for your life.

A Dreaded Mighty Warrior

In any battle, you need to know who you are fighting alongside. Who are your comrades? Who is lending you their strength? Are they faithful? God has painted a picture for you of who He is in battle. When He chose you, He committed Himself to you completely, including in the fight of doubt and discouragement that can occur while waiting for God's words to be fulfilled at the proper time:

> But the LORD is with me as a dread warrior; therefore my persecutors will stumble; they will not overcome me. They will be greatly shamed, for they will not succeed. Their eternal dishonor will never be forgotten.
>
> — Jeremiah 20:11, ESV

When He has decided something in your life, it will be firmly established. There is a certain rest in knowing that, isn't there? He has ordained every victory you will ever need and has lent Himself to stand with you. When He stands, it is as a dreaded warrior. Merriam-Webster's dictionary defines "dread" as, "to be in terror of, to fear intensely, to anticipate with alarm; a source of fear, reverence and awe." God is dreaded because He is Almighty and He is with you, just as He was with Jehoshaphat. No one can withstand His might. No power of hell can stand against Him.

God will help you when the attacks come, but He expects you to suit up with Him for the battle. Like Jehoshaphat, you can wage war with the prophecies.

The Armor of God

As His children, God has given spiritual weapons for a spiritual fight. I love what Paul says about the power behind these spiritual tools:

> The weapons of our warfare are not physical [weapons of flesh and blood]. Our weapons are divinely powerful for the destruction of fortresses. We are destroying sophisticated arguments and every exalted and proud thing that sets itself up against the [true] knowledge of God, and we are taking every thought and purpose captive to the obedience of Christ.
>
> — 2 Corinthians 10:4–5, AMP

That means these spiritual weapons are powered by heaven and God Himself. They are filled with the power of the divine and almighty, powerful God. When the government of the United States sends troops to war, it equips and outfits them with what they need for protection so that they might win the battles that loom ahead. They are issued guns, grenades, knives, night vision goggles, and other regulation items that will sufficiently destroy the threat to the United States of America or the freedom and human rights of others in the world. They are also granted the authority to use these weapons. They are assigned a captain for each team unit.

But you and I are not issued regulation weapons by the US government. Rather, it is the Dreaded Warrior—the Lord of heaven's armies—handing you weapons that come from eternity to defeat your enemies forever. God hands them to you with trust, confidence, and an expectation that they are more than enough to win the battles. These weapons are meant to deal with every argument that might come against your faith in God and His words of promise to you; these are arguments launched by Satan and his cohorts to keep you from your inheritance—from reaching your destiny and fulfilling your assignments. But you have the weapons to beat Satan silly.

Paul gave an incredible description in Ephesians 6:11–17 regarding the power of God, your battle, and your weapons. I'll break down the verses so you are ready to stand firm in the next battle and succeed. But first, digest Ephesians 6:10:

> A final word: Be strong in the Lord and in his mighty power.
> — Ephesians 6:10, NLT

What does it mean to be strong in the Lord and in His mighty power? How does the believer do that? Does he or she act extra tough? Put on a serious demeanor? Swagger cockily around town? No, but it sounds like fun! Paul explained Ephesians 6:10 a little earlier in Ephesians 1:19–20:

> I also pray that you will understand the incredible greatness of God's power for us who believe Him. This is the same mighty power that raised Christ from the dead and seated him in the place of honor at God's right hand in the heavenly realms. (NLT)

God's power is toward us who believe Him. His power toward you is the same kind of power that was toward Jesus—and Jesus faced the greatest battle of all time. Though it appeared to end in death, God's power raised Him from the dead. God wants you to understand that His same power to do what is impossible is available to you in your battles to fulfill His callings. He has more power available to you than what is against you. He has raised you up with His Son Jesus Christ and seated you with Him in heavenly places far above all principalities and powers. He has seated you with Him far above the enemy. He wants to release His power toward you and see you triumph in His promises. It makes Him happy to see you gain the victory.

Be aware of the *kind* of power God possesses to do the impossible. His desire to do the impossible makes you strong in the Lord and in that mighty power. God fights to win, and the battles you are in are to be fought from the place of victory, not toward it. Praise the Lord! How wonderful is God? What mighty weapons and victory are available to believers for every skirmish against their adversary, the devil:

> Put on all of God's armor so that you will be able to stand firm against all strategies of the devil. For we are not fighting against flesh-and-blood enemies, but against evil rulers and authorities of

> the unseen world, against mighty powers in this dark world, and against evil spirits in the heavenly places.
> Therefore, put on every piece of God's armor so you will be able to resist the enemy in the time of evil. Then after the battle, you will still be standing firm. Stand your ground, putting on the belt of truth and the body armor (breastplate) of God's righteousness. For shoes, put on the peace that comes from the Good News so that you will be fully prepared. In addition to all of these, hold up the shield of faith to stop the fiery arrows of the devil. Put on salvation as your helmet, and take the sword of the Spirit, which is the word of God.
>
> — Ephesians 6:11–17, NLT

To stand firm and be immovable, Paul said the believer must wear every single piece of armor. Each piece represents the faithful character of God Himself. God promises those who trust Him will not end up lying half dead, exhausted, or battle-weary somewhere on the battlefield, but rather full of faith and fully celebrating victory with their God.

The Belt of Truth

What is the belt of truth? Who needs a belt in a battle? The soldier's belt held the other armor in place. The belt of truth is the truthfulness of God and it is meant to stabilize and anchor all the other parts of God's spiritual armor. Your God can be trusted for He *is* truth—and this truth is a stabilizing factor. He will not fail you in truthfulness.

King David affirmed this. He wrote, "Behold, You desire truth in the innermost being, And in the hidden part, You will make me know wisdom" (Psalm 51:6). Living in the truth will stabilize your inner man because you are building your life on a firm foundation. This will help you in the battle and keep Satan from attacking your life through sin.

The Breastplate of Righteousness

The body armor of God's righteousness is also called the breastplate of righteousness. It is one of my favorite spiritual weapons. Look at this verse and think carefully about it:

> God made Him who had no sin to be sin for us, so that in him we might become the righteousness of God.
>
> — 2 Corinthians 5:21, NIV

This was the Father's will that His sinless Son would become sin for humanity. The punishment for sin was death, but when Jesus died, that sin was removed; all that is left is perfectly clean righteousness. When the death penalty was paid, God's people were discharged of any wrongdoing. David wrote that, "As far as the east is from the west, so far has He removed our transgressions from us" (Ps. 103:12 NIV).

As I have meditated on this, it has changed my life. I began to view the truth of this Scripture in light of my own sin—God made Jesus who knew no sin to be my sin and then punished the sin. My sin was removed. The righteousness of God, like a clean white robe without spot, was placed on me instead. I became as clean and perfect in righteousness as God is. This gave me much joy and peace. Because all people have sinned, anyone can become a target for the enemy's attack of condemnation, guilt, accusation, and confusion. It is an awful experience. But salvation is a free gift. Gifts are accepted by faith that the one who gave it wants the person to have it and enjoy it. No person can atone for sin by continuing to feel guilty or bad. But if Satan can trick people into feeling bad, he will make them feel like they do not deserve to walk in a victorious life and fulfill their assignments on the earth.

The writer of Hebrews said that not only did Jesus pay for humanity's sin, but, "'Their sins and their lawless deeds I will remember no more.' Where God grants remission of sin there can be no question of making further atonement" (Heb. 10:17–18 Phillips). No further payment or atonement can be made. Your guilt won't pay off what has already been paid. Simply confess and stand firm in the truth that you are not only forgiven, but also righteous and holy. Receive it with a thankful, humble heart. Then, my friend, enjoy it. Enjoy being forgiven.

It's hard to fight battles with your head hung down. God is your glory and the lifter of your head. I used to feel bad, guilty and unworthy all the time. It really held me back from moving forward with my calling to preach, teach, and evangelize. I felt that my motives were never pure enough; there was always something wrong with me. At the rate of trying to get myself together to fulfill my calling, I'd be dead before I got the chance. But God began to teach me that in Jesus alone I was righteous, not in myself. I had a responsibility to allow the Holy Spirit to shape my character, but I also had a responsibility to trust God to shepherd my heart as I moved forward to obey my calling. God wants you to move forward in obedience to Him, standing firm in righteousness, and remain in what I like to call "happy trust." So, chin up and fight the good fight of faith!

The Shoes of the Gospel of Peace.

The Roman soldier's shoes were meant to help him advance. Their soles had cleats in them that make it difficult to retreat. The government of God's kingdom is always advancing and increasing (Isa. 9:6). Jesus commanded His disciples to "Go into all the world and preach the gospel to all creation" (Mark 16:15 NASB), warning that the kingdom of God suffers violence and the violent take it by force (Matt. 11:21). Jesus came to restore this world back into a Garden-of-Eden experience with God, and repair all that was lost. The cross was meant to remove the barrier of sin between man and God, but also to remove the effects of sin.

Sin brought death to man spiritually that eventually played out physically. Sickness is little doses of death that affect parts of the body at an accelerated rate. Injuries are where life is not at full capacity to rejuvenate the body back to wholeness. When Jesus died, it was to restore people's spirit, soul, and body. Sometimes Christians forget to believe Christ for *all* He has done and instead take Him only for the salvation of their souls. That is why so many are depressed, anxious, or sick. But Jesus is able to save the whole of a person's being:

> Now may the God of peace Himself sanctify you entirely; and may your whole spirit, soul and body be preserved without blame at the coming of our Lord Jesus Christ. Faithful is He who calls you, and He also will bring it to pass.
>
> —1 Thessalonians 5:23, NASB

In Isaiah 53, the prophet was clear; the chastisement for peace was on Christ. The punishment was not just for sin but all its effects. Wearing these "shoes" means the child of God advances the kingdom by preaching the full gospel to those God sends them to, but he or she also enforces the gospel's effect to bring full restoration to man. That is why Jesus says that in His name people will, "heal the sick, cleanse the leper, raise the dead and cast out demons" (Matt 10:8, NKJV)

The shoes of the gospel of peace are for you to advance His kingdom in sharing the good news of Jesus, forgiveness, healing, and restoration. Jesus is salvation. He loves every soul He created and wants His children saved—body, soul, and spirit.

The Shield of Faith

Taking up the shield of faith means taking up the character of God in battle. David sang, "Your faithfulness is my shield and buckler." (Ps. 91:4 ESV). But, in the original Hebrew the word "faithfulness" in Psalm 91:4 is derived from the word *aman* (*Strong's* H539). Recall its meaning as "believe, stability, certainty, faithful, established, steadfast, true, permanent, trustworthiness and verity." David is saying the Lord's character is his shield and buckler during attack. When the enemy came in, David relied on the Lord's faithfulness to keep him safe, and so should you.

When the enemy comes in and speaks doubt about God or His promises, raise God's character as your shield.

Remind yourself and the enemy that God is faithful, and He will fulfill His Word and character in your life. Do it out loud if you must. In short order, you will feel full of hope again.

In the heat of battle, a friend of mine would look up to heaven and say, "Oh yeah! I forgot I trust you!" It's simple but I can tell you it works. We can forget in battle that we trust Him. Just lift that shield again where it belongs, with no condemnation, and remember that it is divinely powerful and issued from heaven; His faithfulness cannot fail.

In ancient Roman times, soldiers carried shields to deflect enemy arrows. These shields had leather on them. Soldiers would dip the leather continually in water until it was saturated; thus, the shield would snuff out flaming arrows.

By continually looking at and saturating one's mind with the faithfulness of God's character and committed love, those darts of doubt and unbelief will become easier and easier to quench. A natural shield can become defective with use, but God's faithfulness will never become defective, worn out, or fall into disrepair. Just keep drenching it in His truth.

Dare to be wild and untamable in your faith in Him! Lift that shield of His faithful character with a holy audacity, knowing He is with you, and He will see you through to the victory every time. The more you know God's character, the more joy you can experience in the battle because He cannot fail.

Helmet of Salvation

When the attack comes, it hits the mind first, and often, most of the battle occurs there. The mind is where the battle is won or lost. The examples of battle laid out in Scripture are natural battles but are meant to be applied during spiritual battles. In the Bible, those who won battles were the ones who believed God. They believed His character, they believed Him, and they believed His words and instruction for the battles they were to embark on at His command.

The helmet of salvation protects your mind and thoughts. God's Word declares believers are to be transformed by the renewing of their minds. The world has caused you to think in certain ways from the time you are small. You have been lied to, disappointed, cheated on, and hurt. Sometimes you have done these things to others. These dynamics can become a filter through which God is viewed. Reading the Word will cause you to see God for who He really is and basically brainwash you from the old way of thinking.

When you see how powerful, loving, and committed He is to you, doubts, anxiety, fear, and depression will bounce off your head without injury. Also, the Word will teach you who you are in Christ.[5] As you learn more, that helmet of yours will become thicker and tougher to penetrate. Those attacks will bounce off like a pebble and hit the ground with little to no effect.

I think of Joel Osteen who says something along the lines of, "You are who God says you are, you have every single thing God says you have, and you can do whatever He tells you to do." When I wake up in the morning, I say, "Today, I'm going to think like a saved child of God!" God delights to make us His heirs and co-heirs with Christ. God's faithfulness to you and trust in what He has given you will make your mind peaceful and still, as Isaiah declared: "You will keep him in perfect peace, whose mind is stayed on you for he trusts in you" (Isa. 26:3 ESV).

The Sword of the Spirit

When I think of this piece of the armor of God, I think of the movie Braveheart and William Wallace (Mel Gibson) running into the fight with a battle cry erupting from his heart and mouth.

When you think of the sword of the spirit—the Word of God—do you imagine a sword on your belt? In your hand? I used to as well until I read a few passages that blew my hair back and invigorated me for battle and victory. Look at how John described Jesus in the book of Revelation:

> In his right hand he held seven stars, and coming out of his mouth was a sharp, double-edged sword.
>
> — Revelation 1:19, NIV

John described Jesus with a sharp sword coming out of His mouth with which He strikes down the nations. Jesus uses the Word to slay His adversaries and deal them the death blow with accuracy and with precision.

---

[5] Neil T. Anderson's *Who I am in Christ* is an incredible resource.

The sword of the spirit represents the Word of God, which He has spoken particularly to you by His Spirit for a specific time or situation so it can be used in time of need. The Greek word for this phrase "Word of God" is *rhema* (*Strong's* H4487). The book of Hebrews calls this kind of word living and active and sharper than a two-edged sword (Heb. 4:12). It is "living" because it is filled with the Spirit of life, the Holy Spirit Himself. When Jesus' disciples said to Him, "Only You have the words of life" in John 6:68, this is what they were talking about. When words are inspired by God, they have life within them. The Holy Spirit will speak to your heart and mind words or promises (prophetically or from Scripture) to declare when you are struggling:

> But the Advocate, the Holy Spirit, whom the Father will send in my name, will teach you all things and will remind you of everything I have said to you.
>
> — John 14:26, NASB

How does the Word of life bring death? The Word of life is meant to destroy that which brings death and destruction. It can literally overtake death with life; Isaiah wrote that death is "swallowed up" in victory (Isaiah 25:8). The life of what is right and righteous destroys what is death and not lined up with God.

Using the Sword of the Spirit in Battle

Temptation

One way to use the sword of the Spirit is to fight temptation. Just after Jesus had been baptized by John the Baptist, the Spirit came upon Him. God the Father had just declared Jesus His Beloved Son of whom He well-pleased (Matthew 3:17). Then the Holy Spirit drove Jesus into the wilderness, where He was tempted by the devil for forty days. When severe testing came, He submitted to God and resisted the enemy using words from the Word of God. For example, when the devil tempted Jesus to turn stones into bread Jesus said:

> It is written, Man shall not live by bread alone, but by every word that proceeds from the mouth of God.
>
> — Matthew 4:3–4, NKJV

He used the right word for the right attack, because the Holy Spirit was on Him without measure, speaking to Jesus constantly. Paul the apostle reminds disciples of Jesus in 1 Corinthians 6:17 that, "Those who are joined to the Lord are one spirit with Him." The Holy Spirit is one with you.

Think of the Holy Spirit like coffee. Once cream is added to a cup of coffee, that cream can never be removed. It becomes one with the coffee. You have the Holy Spirit in you and are *one spirit* with Him—and He is just like the Father. He is happy to give you the kingdom (Luke 12:32). This includes a right answer for the devil while experiencing temptation. Submit to God's way, resist the enemy with the sword of the spirit, and hit him hard. He will flee from you. The Holy Spirit will not fail you.

Doubts

The sword can also be used against doubt. Satan has always been standing nearby since chatting with Eve in the garden of Eden, casting doubts about what He has said or about His goodness and faithfulness. These sneaky attacks sound a lot like "Did He really say . . ." or, "How could that ever happen?" or, "You could never . . ."

As you are attacked with a doubt, go back to what God has said to you on the matter and speak it out as a decree. The Holy Spirit is ferocious when it comes to the enemy attacking you with doubt. Let it come up like a battle cry of victory. Speak God's words back to the devil and feel your faith burn like a fire in your chest. Keep at it till he can't stand it anymore.

I remember when I began to feel called to ministry, and a message crossed my path that I knew confirmed it. People also would pray over me and begin to confirm things, often through prophetic words. Once I started preparing for ministry, I began to be hit with doubt. It was horrific, to say the least.

My mind was under constant attack especially as I viewed people around me who had chosen what I would call secure career paths (as if anything could be more secure than God right?). I remember one season when the battle had been nearly unbearable and when God in His mercy spoke to my heart and said, "When did I ever speak to you anything except ministry?"

He had chosen my path, but I had doubted Him. When that happens now, I am much quicker to dismiss the thought as unworthy, or say, "I have made my choice." I simply remember that I was called, and I know I would not be happy doing anything else. Then I declare God's Word against the enemy as a sword.

Waging War with the Prophecies

Now that you are suited up in your armor and strengthened in the character of God, you're ready to go to wage war with the prophecies. The prophetic Word is simply when a word comes to you directly from God or through another as one of God's mouthpieces. It can also come in other forms, based on Scripture, such as dreams and visions (consider Joseph's dream in Genesis 37). Regardless of the avenue, the prophetic Word is a powerful weapon. It is a word of life and filled with the Spirit's power.

When God gives you a clear word, it is meant to be a sword in your mouth that combats doubts. It is a divine weapon. God has made His plans clear to you; your job is to hold your ground for that piece of the kingdom.

Advance in Prayer

One way to advance—to wage war with the prophecies— is through prayer. Jeremiah the prophet had told Israel that the nation would be in bondage for seventy years. Remember that God does nothing without first telling the prophets (Amos 3:7). After many warnings and encouragements to repent and turn to God, Israel ended up in exile because they did not heed those warnings. Daniel was a young man who was taken into that exile, but his heart was fastened to God. While in exile toward the later part of his life he was reading the words of Jeremiah the prophet:

> It was the first year of the reign of Darius the Mede, the son of Ahasuerus, who became king of the Babylonians. During the first year of his reign, I, Daniel, learned from reading the word of the Lord, as revealed to Jeremiah the prophet, that Jerusalem must lie desolate for seventy years. So I turned to the Lord God and pleaded with him in prayer and fasting. I also wore rough burlap and sprinkled myself with ashes.
>
> — Daniel 9:1–3, NLT

Daniel learned from reading Jeremiah that Israel's captivity would last seventy years. Why did Daniel pray and fast? The answer is found in Psalm 115:16. It'll fire you up as you look at it in light of waging war for your own family or life. David wrote that, "The highest heavens belong to the LORD, but the earth he has given to mankind."

That word "given" is the key word! It is the Hebrew word *nathan* (*Strong's* H5414) which means, "assigned, committed, charged, distributed and granted." When the Godhead created man, even though God owned the earth, He assigned dominion of the earth to mankind and gave it to them to rule and govern. Think of a landlord. He owns the home but when he has rented it out, he can no longer go in and out of the house whenever he wants. The house is under the authority of the tenant. The tenant, at that point, must invite the landlord to enter the home. It is the same with God. Jesus taught His disciples this concept when He instructed them to pray after they had asked for teaching in that area (Luke 11, Matt. 6:5). He said to ask God to bring His kingdom to come on the earth and His will to be done on the earth as it is in heaven. Even the Son of God followed this pattern of understanding. The prophet Daniel understood this, too. He knew the prophetic Word and prayed that the Kingdom of God would come, and the will of God would be done on the earth as it is in heaven—and it was.

Recall that words have creative power and they are seeds. Wise King Solomon warned to be careful what you sow because you will have to eat the fruit of it (Prov. 18:21). I remember hearing a speaker say that the only antidote to a lie is truth. Stand firm regarding what God has spoken and make up your mind to believe it. When we speak God's words, it is His voice and it's powerful. Look at this incredible Psalm David wrote under the inspiration of the Holy Spirit:

> The voice of the Lord is powerful;
> The voice of the Lord is full of majesty.
> The voice of the Lord breaks the cedars,
> The voice of the Lord shakes the wilderness;
> The voice of the Lord makes the deer give birth,
> And strips the forests bare.
>
> — Psalm 29:4, 5, 8, 9, NLT

The Lord's voice is over creation and all circumstances, and when He speaks there is a response because He is power. His voice in the spirit realm breaks, shakes, and births things in the natural realm. Soon you will see His power evidenced in your life.

Remember that His words in your mouth have the same power as His Word in *His* mouth. Think of a messenger who goes out into the kingdom and proclaims the edict of a decree of the king. Under assignment of the king, the word in his mouth has the same force of law as it does in the king's mouth. So, speak up! Don't hold back, don't hold your tongue, and don't be shy or timid. Having done all to stand, my friend, stand firm (Eph. 6:13).

Decree

There is incredible power in decrees when God speaks to you regarding any aspect of your life. Although I have never been to YWAM (Youth With a Mission), I have sat under their teaching many times and utilized it in my life and in my family's life. One of the best testimonial books I have read on hearing God's voice is *Is That Really You, God?* by Lorne Cunningham, YWAM's founder. It is filled with God's presence and practical, faith-filled obedience.

Interestingly, God told Cunningham to buy the Hotel Golf in Munich for mission work. So, he and his team declared that word out loud. Cunningham wrote:

> I set my mind and spirit never to doubt that the necessary money would be there, and on time . . . On the very last day, the money was due, we were still lacking $10,000. I went to the post office to check our mail one last time before going to give our payment. There, waiting in our box, were donations from several people who believed in what we were doing. I found it very hard to believe—the total was $10,060! Just out of curiosity, I watched the box for four days after we had paid the full amount, but nothing came in—not a dime.[6]

Cunningham's story illustrates the power of agreeing with God—the power of decreeing what God says, speaking that word out loud, and standing firm. Remember God's Word declares in Psalm 24:1 that "The earth is the Lord's, and everything in it. The world and all its people belong to him."

God has the right to issue the decree of His will. But He has given it to man to steward and govern. The Hebrew word "decree" is *choq* (*Strong's* H2706), and is defined as "a statute, ordinance, due law, appointed, rule and set time and task." Webster's dictionary defines it as "an order having the force of law, a foreordaining will <God's will>, an order or decision given by a person or group in authority."[7] It is meant to convey edict, commandment, mandate, and proclaim by order of a governing authority. David illustrates this saying:

> I will proclaim the Lord's decree:
> He said to me, "You are my son;
> today I have become your father.
> Ask me, and I will make the nations your inheritance,
> the ends of the earth your possession."
>
> — Psalm 2:7, NIV

---

[6] Cunningham, Loren with Rogers, Janice, *Is That Really You, God*? YWAM Publishing, United States 2015
[7] www.merriam-webster.com "decree" (Jan. 17, 2017).

God's authority is absolute, but He shares it with man. The earth He has given and assigned to the children of men (Ps. 115:16 NKJV). Believers can take that decree and issue it through their governing authority; as stewards, they can speak it on the earth as it is in heaven as a statute, ordinance, or set time, and task with governing authority.

Why Do Decrees Work?

Reinhard Bonnke tells a powerful story about a time he was preparing in the afternoon for a gospel crusade in Africa. The Holy Spirit revealed to him the connection between God's Word and God's power released through the person of the Holy Spirit. God directed him to Genesis:

> In the beginning, God created the heavens and the earth. The earth was without form and void, and darkness was over the face of the deep. And the Spirit of God was hovering over the face of the waters. And God said, "Let there be light," and there was light.
>
> — Genesis 1:1–3, ESV

The Holy Spirit was hovering and brooding over a vast, dark void without any form—without any order. The Spirit was waiting for the Word of God to be released. God's will is in His very words. The Holy Spirit was the power to make it so. God spoke to that which was not as though it was, and it then existed. When God reveals what His plan or desire is on a situation, speak it out. Release it. The Holy Spirit is hovering and waiting with power to make it so. So, speak out God's promises over your mountains, over your kids, and over your community—everything to which God has assigned you spiritual responsibility.

Waging War with Governing Prayer

Now, when God gives you a word of promise or an assignment, it is up to you to govern heaven and Earth with it. He has given you something without regret and without repentance. He will not take it back. With it comes an incredible amount of authority believers rarely tap into. Meditate on these Scriptures for a few moments:

> I will give him the key to the house of David—the highest position in the royal court. When he opens doors, no one will be able to close them; when he closes doors, no one will be able to open them. He will bring honor to his family name, for I will drive him firmly in place like a nail in the wall. They will give him great responsibility, and he will bring honor to even the lowliest members of his family.
>
> — Isaiah 22:22–24, NLT

God is trying to help you understand what level of authority you have when you have a word or assignment. You have been given your position by the King who has all authority in the kingdom! Look at what the New Bible Commentary says:

> The key of David comes in this context of accountability. A key was a substantial object, tucked in the girdle or slung on the shoulder, but the opening words of v.22 with their echo that went with it, to be used in the king's interests. The "shutting" and "opening" means the power to make decisions which no one under the king could override.[8]

These keys, worn on the shoulder, were objects of governance. The keys permitted access or denied it. When God gives you something, He has given you authority to make decisions in the spiritual and natural realm regarding that which has been entrusted to you. No one under the King can override it. This is known as "governing prayer."

In Isaiah 9:6 the prophet declared that the Messiah would carry the government on His shoulders and of the increase of His kingdom there will be no end.

---

[8] Intervarsity Press, *The New Bible Commentary* Grand Rapids: Wm. B. Eerdmans Publishing Co, 1991

Jesus was given all authority in heaven and on Earth and what doors He opens no man can close and what doors He closes no man can open (Rev. 3:7–8). In turn, He has given these keys to you. Matthew described this same idea symbolized in Matthew 16:16–19 as the keys of the kingdom of heaven:

> Simon Peter answered, "You are the Messiah, the Son of the living God." Jesus replied, "Blessed are you, Simon son of Jonah, for this was not revealed to you by flesh and blood, but by my Father in heaven. And I tell you that you are Peter, and on this rock I will build my church, and the gates of Hades will not overcome it. I will give you the keys of the kingdom of heaven; whatever you bind on earth will be bound in heaven, and whatever you loose on earth will be loosed in heaven." (NIV)

This idea of "governing prayer" is seen in the Old Testament through Elijah, the prophet of God, sent to turn Israel back to her heavenly Father. In the assignment, he was given authority by the Lord, the King of the universe. Elijah said, "As surely as the Lord lives—the God I serve—there shall be neither dew nor rain these years, except by my word" (1 Kings 17:1 NASB).

Elijah did not permit the heavens to release rain until his people repented for their idolatry and turned to God. God complied, for He is the one who gave Elijah the assignment and established him in such a high position.

Joshua was another example of someone who used his authority on an assignment. God had told Joshua to go into battle and sent hailstones and confusion to the enemy. Joshua knew he had the victory for God had promised it, but the day was ending. He did not want to leave the battle partly won—he was after the whole victory—so he commanded the sun to stop. Joshua 10:14 says that Lord listened to the voice of a man, and indeed the sun continued to shine. God had submitted Himself to the governance of the one He gave the assignment to: Joshua.

God wants you to speak and govern your assignments as interests for the King, too. He said in Isaiah, "I have put My words in your mouth and have covered you with the palm of my hand, to establish the heavens and to found the earth" (Isaiah 51:16 NASB).

What you decide on the earth will be established in heaven. Understanding that the King of the universe has all authority and has given it to you will result in serving Him with an established, steadfast, and single-minded heart. You have an assignment—govern it! Decide now, using your authority by faith, and win it!

Access to the Treasuries

Seven times Jesus declared in Scripture that those who ask according to His will have fullness of joy. When followers of Jesus ask according to *His* will, as the words Jesus speaks are according to God's will, He will do it. First John 5:14 encourages believers to take confidence in this: "If we ask anything in His will, He hears us, and we have the petition we ask of Him." Tim Perrine wrote in his book *Kneeling Christian*:

> Blessed be the God and Father of our Lord Jesus Christ, who has blessed us with every spiritual blessing in the Heavenly places in Christ (Eph. 1:3). God's great storehouse is full of blessings. Only prayer (asking) can unlock that storehouse. Prayer is the key, and faith turns the key and claims the blessings.[9]

You have a Father who desires to give you the kingdom and a Savior who died to make you an heir and co-heir with Him. He has given you the keys of the kingdom and access to His treasuries. You have all you need to wage war, fight the good fight, and "get 'er done" with confidence.

Reflect with the Holy Spirit

Ask the Holy Spirit to reveal Himself as the Dreaded Warrior by contemplating the following questions. Consider that He might be calling you to learn how

[9] Perrine, Tim "*Kneeling Christian*" Christian Classics Ethereal Library. http://www.ccel.org/ccel/unknown/kneeling.html (Jan.12, 2017)

to fight the battles in your life with His power. Remember: He has given you the authority to complete any assignments He gives you!

1. Lord, show me how You view the armor You have given me, and how You want me to utilize that power better—and in what areas of my life. ____

   ____

   ____

2. How do You see me in the assignments You have given me?

   ____

   ____

3. What have You promised me? What have You assigned to me?

   ____

   ____

4. What am I battling right now? ______________________________

   ____

   ____

5. Is there anything in this chapter, Lord, that You really want me to learn and remember? ______________________________

   ____

   ____

6. How is my faith developing? ______________________________

   ____

   ____

7. What do I need to access in Your treasure house?______________

   ____

8. Is there anything special You want to share with me?___________

    ____

    ____

CHAPTER 13 – BELIEVE WITH YOUR SILENCE OR YOUR WORDS

Death and life are in the power of the tongue, And those who love it will eat its fruit. — Proverbs 18:21, NKJV

Believe with Your Mouth

When God created you, He made you in His own image. This means literally a phantom image, a likeness so profound that it lends credence to the phrase, "Like father, like son." He made you with the same ability to create reality around you with words. Proverbs 18:21 says, "Death and life are in the power of the tongue, and those who love it will eat its fruits" (NKJV).

Have you ever listened to someone constantly complain and say terrible things about a spouse, children, job, or life? Their words have a defeating and often gross and defiling "feel" to them. Perhaps you have watched their situation continue to stay the same or grow worse year after year. In all creation, human beings alone have creative power in their tongues. Words are little seeds that go forth and produce a fruit or harvest into the natural realm. This is in the likeness of God's power—and with it comes an outstanding opportunity, incredible privilege, and a tremendous responsibility.

This chapter will discuss two ways to be wise in using this powerful likeness: believing with your silence or believing with your words—and both are an important way to believe and trust God. Let's first revisit the word "believe." To "believe" means, "to be firm, endure, be faithful, fidelity, be true, stand fast, trust, quiet, free from argument or objection, fixed, fastened, established." Your words need to line up with God's promises, with faithfulness and fidelity. There must be no cheating with the "mistress of doubt;" you must be free from argument, and quietly trusting in God.

God has given your words power and authority. If you are in the heat of the battle and are struggling to keep your words in line with God's, the other option is silence. Staying silent is a great way to keep yourself from working against God's great plan, protecting it from the wrong kind of words. Let's look at a few examples God has laid out in His word to help you understand this and win the battle for your destiny.

Silent Faith

Zechariah and Elizabeth

When God chose to send Jesus to the earth, He needed to send someone to announce His arrival, John the Baptist, and prepare the people for a change. A new covenant after 2,000 years is a big deal. It would shift history, culture, status of various people groups, and even the status of the nations of the earth. Instead of Israel being God's chosen people, all nations would have access to God through Jesus.

God selected Elizabeth and Zechariah, a couple that was righteous before Him, but sadly they were barren and well advanced in years. While Zechariah was ministering to the Lord in the temple, the angel Gabriel appeared to him and announced that God was answering his prayers for a son. This son would prepare the way for the Lord's coming. Unfortunately, Zechariah responded by using that little tongue of his to send forth the first word of doubt and death into God's perfect will by saying:

> How can I be sure this will happen? I'm an old man now, and my wife is also well along in years.
>
> — Luke 1:18, NLT

He didn't ask how it would happen like his little cousin Mary who was going to birth Jesus. He asked how he could be *sure* it would happen. See the difference? Israel knew God only by His *acts*; Moses, however, knew God by His *ways*—His character. Moses was confident God's character would manifest in faithful action. Israel, on the other hand, needed constant signs to be sure that God was faithful. Can you see it here with Zechariah? Doubt! This could seriously mess up everything. The angel, acting as God's messenger, promptly put a stop to the issue saying:

> I am Gabriel! I stand in the very presence of God. It was He who sent me to bring you this good news! But now, since you didn't believe what I said, you will be silent and unable to speak until the child is born. For my words will certainly be fulfilled in the proper time.
>
> — Luke 1:19–20, NLT

Zechariah was rendered mute until he named the baby "John" at the circumcision ceremony. God was not going to allow the power of Zechariah's words to speak death to His plans. Zechariah's words of doubt and unbelief, spoken into the situation, invited the whole world to eat the fruit of those little doubt seeds. If Zechariah's words would not line up and agree with God, then his silence would. Once those words were uttered, they could not be taken back. God had to perform them. He wasn't going to change His mind. And believing means belief without argument, free from objection, and in quietness. Sometimes God will shut His children up for their own good. Faith is speaking according to God's reality, not ours.

One of the ways I have noticed God silence unbelief and fear in my life and in others' lives is by hardening the hearts of my friends to my plights. They begin to drop away for a season or aren't interested in talking about my challenges or listening to me complain about them. Believe it or not, this can be an act of the mercy of God to keep you on track to your destiny. When there's nobody to talk to and complain to, then there are no words of unbelief to keep you from reshaping God's plan for your life or aborting it all together.

If you are struggling to speak the truth, try being quiet instead. Don't talk about it, but rather worship and praise God.

Joshua and Caleb

When the children of Israel were given the Promised Land, they sent twelve spies to check out the land. Ten of them brought back a report contrary to God's and told everyone that they could not defeat the giants. Two men, however—Joshua and Caleb—gave a report about God's faithfulness. If God said they could take the land, then they could! Sadly, the children of Israel did not believe the good report but instead believed the bad one. They were free from objection or argument to the bad report. They trusted it with fidelity . . . and sadly, they died in the wilderness while God raised a new generation.

God raised a new generation because He had promised to give the land to Israel, which required Him to follow through and not change His mind. God waited for a new generation that would not personally associate with unbelief.

This new generation's dissociation with unbelief helped the nation of Israel cross the Jordan supernaturally through faith in a good God who had upheld and loved it for forty years in the wilderness. Next, God gave instructions for taking Jericho. The Israelites were to walk around the city's walls silently for seven days. The nation's people had the power in their words to undo God's plans again. So, God was careful to instruct a great silence over the people. Walking around a city and looking at its incredible walls, can cause some doubt. . . and Jesus taught, "Out of the abundance of the heart, the mouth speaks" (Luke 6:45 NKJV).

It is best to "zip the lip" in times when obstacles feel greater than your faith. When things grow tough, let your silence believe quietly and with fidelity toward God's faithfulness.

Spoken Faith

Zerubbabel

Zechariah was a prophet of God who lived during the time Judah had just returned from exile in Babylon. God had sent Judah to Babylon as a disciplinary action to soften her heart back to Him and away from idols. The people returned home to a devastated land and a destroyed temple. God sent young Zechariah to encourage Zerubbabel, the governor of Judah, and the people of Judah in the work of restoring the temple and rebuilding the Jewish nation. Zerubbabel faced much opposition to the Lord's work, which led to discouraged apathy and long periods of halted work. The vision waned and the nation began to wither as its hope dried up. But God works everything together for good for those who love Him (Rom. 8:28). He knows exactly what to do with dry seasons. No one saw it coming, but God released a holy fire in Zechariah who cried out the Word of the Lord:

> Who are you, O great mountain?
> Before Zerubbabel, you shall become a plain!
> And he shall bring forth the capstone
> With shouts of "Grace, grace to it!"
> Moreover, the word of the Lord came to me, saying:
> "The hands of Zerubbabel
> Have laid the foundation of this temple:
> His hands shall also finish it."
>
> — Zechariah 4:6–10, NKJV

I love God's perspective of the obstacles. He questioned the "mountain's" (the obstacle's) audacity to stand up against Zerubbabel. When God chose Zerubbabel for the work, he was on a God-assignment. No one and nothing is greater than God; no authority is higher. Therefore, no obstacle had any right to stand against God's appointed worker. Zechariah, the prophet, was to speak that perspective boldly, out loud, to shift the people's mindset to the authority of the God of heaven and Earth, and to His assigned worker. He then spoke to the obstacle that stood before Zerubbabel and commanded it to become a level plain. Zerubbabel was to lay the foundation by cooperating with God, shouting, "Grace, grace to it!" (Zech. 4:7 NKJV).

Imagine shouting the Word of the Lord over the assignments God has given you. Does it seem uncomfortable? Imagine how Zerubbabel felt—everyone with their tools standing by, moms and babies and merchants watching and listening. But Zerubbabel's loyalty was to God, not to man. He had a choice: he could line up his fidelity, faithfulness, and tongue to the Lord his God and shout the supernatural grace and favor of God over his work, or he could go back to apathy and defeat. But he couldn't do both. He obeyed and spoke God's Word, trusting in the Lord to make it so. His words cooperated with God's words, power was released, and the work was completed.

God also had a message for the people of Israel. By the word of the Lord, no one was to despise the day of small beginnings (Zech. 4:10). Everyone may have seen Zerubbabel start, but God saw him finish. God knows the end from the beginning. The Israelites were to keep God's perspective and line up their vision with His, because out of their mouths their hearts would speak (Luke 6:45). God did not want unbelief for His people or the discouragement that comes with it, but rather faith. By believing God's words and seeing God's vision, their words could cooperate with God's and join in building the destiny of the nation.

It is the same for God's children today, who must line up their vision with His and speak out in agreement; they must let their words believe. Fight against being double-minded, believing one minute and doubting the next. It is exhausting, confusing, and devastating to your peace and well-being. It creates a back and forth tug of war. Trust can be one of the most powerful forces you will ever know. When you believe God's goodness, faithfulness, and words, you will experience rest for your soul. Speak the word of the Lord to every obstacle in your life with a faithfulness to God.

Abraham

Abram (later named Abraham) and Sarai (later named Sarah) were infertile their whole lives as a couple. God had promised them a son and they thought they had helped God with His plan by having Abram sleep with Hagar, Sarai's servant. After all, God did not declare Sarai would produce the heir until after the little plot they hatched had been completed. You can almost hear them cheering, "We did it! We made it happen!" Interestingly, heaven is silent on the matter until God appeared again to Abram many years later in a vision with the intention of making a covenant, which would promise him countless descendants:

> I will make a covenant with you, by which I will guarantee to give you countless descendants."
> At this, Abram fell face down on the ground. Then God said to him, "This is my covenant with you: I will make you the father of a multitude of nations! What's more, I am changing your name. It will no longer be Abram. Instead, you will be called Abraham, for you will be the father of many nations. I will make you extremely fruitful. Your descendants will become many nations, and kings will be among them!" Then God said to Abraham, "Regarding Sarai, your wife—her name will no longer be Sarai. From now on her name will be Sarah. And I will bless her and give you a son from her! Yes, I will bless her richly, and she will become the mother of many nations. Kings of nations will be among her descendants."
>
> — Genesis 17:2–7, NLT

God's word had gone out and it had power in it to create something out of nothing. When God changed Abram and Sarai's names, He changed their identities.

Abram had to tell everyone to start to call him Abraham – father of nations, as an old man. Sarai had to do the same as an old woman—a mother of nations. How awkward that must have been! But God had a destiny for them as a couple, so view this from God's perspective. When Abraham and Sarah cooperated with God in obedience and faith, they caused everyone else to be active participators in God's plan. If God's Word does not return void (Isa. 55:11), and people were repeating it, then they were seeding His Word over and over and over. In 2 Corinthians 13:1 Paul wrote that by the mouths of two or three witnesses every word is established. Abraham was counted as a prophet by God, and he spoke God's words as God's mouthpiece. When a person spoke his or Sarah's name, that person stood in agreement with God and spoke His word over and over as a prophetic echo—making themselves mouthpieces over this prophetic destiny for all time. God is merciful and wonderful to include so many in His plans to speak over Abraham and Sarah. The destiny of the world was forever changed by each person who spoke God's word, but it started with Abram's gutsy obedience to change his and Sarai's name.

When you look at a seed and see only one, you are seeing with limitation. Instead, when you look at a seed, imagine how many trees are in that seed. This acknowledges God's limitless vision and mindset. Look at your life with Jesus. Look at who He says you are and look at what you sense He is asking you to do on this earth—and begin believing with your words. They are seeds, they are life, they are eternal, and they are born of love. They will never return void.

Recall once again Jehoshaphat who announced back to God His awesome blessings and promises:

> O our God, did you not drive out those who lived in this land when your people Israel arrived? And did you not give this land forever to the descendants of your friend Abraham?
>
> — 2 Chronicles 20:7, NLT

He knew that when God granted a blessing, it was an eternal blessing. God would not take it back. Jehoshaphat was greatly rewarded for keeping his words and faith in line with God's. The nation of Israel won its battle of faith and continued to live in the land God swore to give its people forever. And it will be exactly the same with you. If you do what they did, you will get what they got!

Reflect with the Holy Spirit:

Welcome Jesus into the following questions and listen to His thoughts:

1. Would You like me to change any of my words in an area of my life? What can I say differently, Lord? ______________________

   ____

   ____

2. When was the last time I sensed You speaking and had faith and assurance it would be done? ______________________________

____

____

3. Is there anything You are asking me to begin to say by faith and trust to seed Your plans for my life? Or to seed Your plans for others? ____

____

____

4. Would You like me to remain silent about anything? __________

____

____

5. Lord, help me be willing to embrace the awkwardness between agreeing with what You have announced over me and what others will not see before it manifests. How can I prepare myself for that? Make me bold and strengthen my soul to go through to victory.

____

____

6. When have I blessed You with my words, Lord, and made You smile? ____

____

____

7. Am I feeling more bold and full of faith? Do I have a greater sense of adventure? ____

____

____

Chapter 14 – Believe with Thanks and Praise

Now thanks be to God who always leads us in triumph in Christ, and through us diffuses the fragrance of His knowledge in every place.
— 2 Corinthians 2:14, NKJV

Look at the above verse carefully. Chew on the words. Absorb its full flavor. *Always. Triumph.* Words like these embolden the child of God. It is God who leads you in triumph, and He is a God that knows no defeat. When does He do it? Always! What a promise! He wins every battle every time. No wonder Paul encouraged followers of Jesus to give thanks. God's plan for you is to experience victory in every area of your life and He's willing to do His part to get you there; your part is trusting with praise and thanks.

Seeing the Present with the End in Mind

As you praise and thank Jesus in the face of trials, you are trusting that He can and will work things out for good for you and others (Rom 8:28).

Corrie ten Boom tells a story of a young lady she met in Africa during one of her many evangelistic travels. The young lady was a missionary and had many children. Having children in Africa at that time meant sending them to a missionary school when they reached school age. The young mother discovered that she was pregnant again and was devastated and angry with God, knowing she had another child she would have to give up.

Eventually, the day came to go to the hospital to give birth. They loaded up all the children and made the long drive to the hospital. She gave birth to a beautiful baby girl. When they returned home, they learned that the day she had gone to the hospital, a renegade tribe went through the whole area and killed every single white person. If they had been home, even their little children would have been massacred. She told Corrie that the gift she had complained about had saved her family's life. She learned to give thanks, to praise and to trust that God saw what was happening before she did. Though the present situation may have looked dismal, God had a beautiful end in mind.

Return your mind once again to Jehoshaphat. He shared this same understanding as Paul and faced his trial with thanks and praise, modelling this attitude to his people. Through his experience, Jehoshaphat teaches believers today how they, too, can approach a battle through the lens of God's love and character, keeping the end – the victory – in mind:

> After consulting the people, the king appointed singers to walk ahead of the army, singing to the Lord and praising Him for His holy splendor. This is what the sang: "Give thanks to the Lord; His faithful love endures forever!"
>
> — 2 Chronicles 20:21, NLT

God's great plan for you to be at peace in your life is not based on circumstances. That is why Jesus said, "Peace I give to you, not as the world gives do I give to you" (John 14:27 NKJV). People generally experience peace in the world when their circumstances are good, and all their ducks are in a row. But the reality is, nobody's ducks are ever in row! Sometimes, they are not even on the pond. There will always be trials, and it's important to understand there is no triumph without a trial. God knows difficulties will come. However, instead of being the enemy of your soul, difficulties can become your best friend as they teach the power of His great character. You will then emerge on the other side of the battle in victory.

His Banner, Your Battle Cry

King Solomon wrote in Songs 2:4, "He brought me to the banqueting-house, and his banner over me was love." The English word "banqueting" in Hebrew is the word *yayin*, or "wine." (*Strong's* H3196). Thus, His "banqueting house" means "house of wine." Wine represents the covenant with God through blood and sacrifice. The Hebrew word for "banner" is *degel* (*Strong's* H1714), which means "a flag or a standard." Banners represented a king, his country, his culture, and his citizens. Kings would issue a decree that would act as a covering stating that all beneath that "banner" were under the authority of that king, kingdom, and the king's edict. Banners proclaimed to anyone who could see, including the king's enemies, what the kingdom stood for.

Banners were also a rallying point for war; they went *before* an army. Israel fought under and behind the banner of God, as God's soldiers fighting for the will of God to prevail on the earth and in the destiny of His people. God's love was toward them, unfailing and undefeatable because God is undefeatable. His love endures forever because He is eternal.

As *your* banner, God proclaims to you, your enemies, and those around you that His banner is love and that love will never fail you. You are a citizen of God's kingdom and have all the rights and privileges that go with that citizenship. Look at a banqueting moment that David described:

> You prepare a table before me in the presence of my enemies.
> You anoint my head with oil; my cup overflows.
> Surely your goodness and love will follow me all the days of my life,
> and I will dwell in the house of the Lord forever.
>
> — Psalm 23:5–6, NIV

Imagine the Lord has prepared a banquet with all your favorite foods. You are humbled and amazed as you sit down to eat. You look up and above you there is a satin banner shimmering against the candlelight from the table. In bold lettering, it reads, "Unfailing Love." It is only over your seat. Your emotions are thick and your heart swells within your chest. You are anticipating an intimate dinner with Him. You wait for the Lord to sit down, but He doesn't. He walks over to the door and opens it. Your heart races as you watch your enemies come into the banqueting hall one by one.

Hostility begins to fill the room and you feel your peace dissipating. The Lord allows your enemies to sit at your table and bids you to eat. You hardly know what to think but you trust Him and begin to savor the food. Slowly you allow yourself to rest and enjoy despite the hostility. He's right there.

Then the Lord does something. A hush fills the hall as He takes out His oil and anoints your head and no one else's. He smiles. He has demonstrated His favor. You feel courage rising within you. He looks up at the banner over you and looks each of your enemies in the eye and says, "Unfailing Love." His voice is filled with resolve. They get the message. If they come after you, His love will not fail you. They will be defeated because He will fight with you in the battle.

He has done something far greater than dining with you. He has taught you to rest and enjoy the meal and His company in the middle of adversity, because He has openly declared a forever victory over you. Your battle cry is that cry of unfailing love, and it resonates from deep within. It's a shout of victory prior to battle, knowing that the one who gave up His life will surely give you victory as you trust in Him.

God Speaks Personally

One morning I was meditating on the Scripture, "His banner over me is love" (Songs 2:4 NASB) and the Lord spoke to me and said, "God is love. Love is a person and love never fails. I am Love and I cannot fail you. I am undefeatable! My love endures forever, long after your enemies and their plans have passed. My love goes through everything you go through and will not yield." Only hours later, I received an email from a person I did not know stating that God is Jehovah-Nissi. Translated to English, this phrase means, "God is my banner." I knew God was trying to capture my attention, so I looked up the passage from Exodus 17. Whatever He was saying, I wanted all of it in my life and I knew He wanted it in the lives of the body of Christ.

The passage described how the Amalekites attacked Israel, and how Moses commanded Joshua to prepare for battle. Moses would stand at the top of a nearby hill and hold out the staff of God over the battle. Aaron and Hur held up his hands as the battle waged on. At the end of a long day of fighting, the Israelites had secured the victory. They viewed it in the moment as a "now" victory, but God viewed it *over generations* saying:

> "Write this down on a scroll as a permanent reminder, and read it aloud to Joshua: I will erase the memory of Amalek from under heaven." Moses built an altar there and named it Yahweh-Nissi (which means "the Lord is my banner"). He said, "They have raised their fist against the Lord's throne, so now the Lord will be at war with Amalek generation after generation."
>
> — Exodus 17:14–15, NLT

God's commitment and faithfulness to His people will outlast any problem at hand. Man thinks in the mindset of moments, but God thinks in the mindset of eternity. He is your banner and He lives forever.

When enemies come against you and your destiny, they have raised a fist against God's throne. The kingdom of God suffers violence, but the violent take it by force (Matt. 11:12). Gather yourself and your strength under the rallying point for war, your banner—God. He will endure long after your battle and will continue your victory long after you have walked off the battlefield. No wonder His people can praise Him continually and sing ahead of their battles!

The Best Example of Praise

Praise is a declaration of the attributes of God; it is a display and celebration of who He is. Jehoshaphat went into battle praising the Lord, sending the worshippers first and the army second. That is because Jehoshaphat counted God's love faithful and trusted Him with his obedience, declaring, "Give thanks to the Lord for His faithful love endures forever" (2 Chron. 20:21 NLT)

Recall that God inhabits the praises of His people (Ps. 22:3) and that the word "inhabits" in Hebrew is *yashab* (*Strong's* H3427) means, "to sit down (specifically as a judge) like a throne or judgment seat within, to wait and make ambush against." Each definition above applies. Remember, God set up an ambush in the unseen realm and judged between the enemy and Jehoshaphat and destroyed Jehoshaphat's oppressors. The sentence was death. The battlefield was later renamed, "The Field of Blessing." For your enemies, the place of conflict will be named the place of death—but for you, it will be a field of blessing. It will be a testimony to the greatness of your covenant God and His enduring love.

Look at Abijah's fight in 2 Chronicles 13. Jeroboam was a usurper to the throne of Israel. He was Solomon's servant. God had made a covenant with David that his descendants would sit on the throne forever. That means the usurper was temporary and not someone who could partake of the promises. Jeroboam had also chased away God's priests and led people into idol worship. Jeroboam wanted more territory and went after Abijah, David's great-grandson and king of Judah. But Abijah was confident, even though he only boasted 400,000 men to Jeroboam's 800,000. He tried to warn Jeroboam, saying:

> "Do you really think you can stand up against the kingdom of the Lord that is led by the descendants of David? You may have a vast army, and you have those golden calves that Jeroboam made as your gods . . . But as for us, the Lord is our God and we have not abandoned Him . . . So you see, God is with us. He is our leader. His priests will blow their trumpets and lead us into battle against you. O people of Israel, do not fight against the Lord, the God of your ancestors. You will not succeed."
>
> — 2 Chronicles 13:8, 10, 12, NLT

Jeroboam made a sneaky move and set up an ambush behind Abijah. Abijah's men cried out to God. The Levites (the priests) knew exactly how to approach God. They sounded a victorious blast on their trumpets and the men responded:

> When Judah realized that they were being attacked from the front and the rear, they cried out to the Lord for help.
> Then the priests blew the trumpets, and the men of Judah began to shout. At the sound of their battle cry, God defeated Jeroboam and all Israel and routed them before Abijah and the army of Judah.
>
> — 2 Chronicles 14:14-16, NLT

That word "shout" in Hebrew is *ruwa* (*Strong's* H7321), the same word for "battle cry." It means, "to mar especially by breaking, to split the ear, shout for joy, alarm, and destroy, to make a joyful noise, rejoicing triumph." This is the same word used in Psalm 47:1 where David declared, "Shout to the Lord with a voice of triumph." This shout/battle cry was one of praise, victory, trust, and worship. God inhabited their praise and destroyed the enemy and Jeroboam, who lost 500,000 men that day. That was more than Judah's entire army. The victory their praise wrought was forever recorded in 2 Chronicles: "So Judah defeated Israel on that occasion because they trusted in the Lord, the God of their ancestors (2 Chron. 13:18 NLT).

Abijah and his men trusted with their praise. They stood firm and engaged with God in a joyful battle cry proclaiming that they (and He) could not be defeated.

Your Personal Battle Cry

The love that drove Jesus to the cross is the battle cry of your life. If He died for you, He will give you everything else. Paul reasoned that what Jesus did flowed from this love, and it beseeches believers to do the same:

> He who did not spare his own Son, but gave him up for us all- how will he not also, along with Him freely give us all things.
>
> — Romans 8:32, NIV

You can face every battle with praise. He has given you His Son, and His love is your battle cry as well. You can praise with confidence in that love. Nothing can stand against God and nothing is impossible with Him. He is Lord over every circumstance, boss, child, addiction, marriage issue, financial mess, wound, ministry, or relationship.

Look at everything you are facing and decide today to believe that God's banner and declaration over you is love. Release your battle cry of praise and victory to the Lord over it in Jesus' name. Let Him inhabit your praises and judge on your behalf.

A New Testament of Praise

The beauty of the Lord is that He is the same yesterday, today and forever (Heb. 13:8). God's character is in no way an Old Testament reality. It is a "God Almighty reality" and it holds true for as long as God exists—which is forever.

This is played out again in the New Testament as Paul and Silas were put in jail after ministering in the city of Philippi. However, they understood their hope and held their joy. All ears were on them as they did the incredible. From their prison cell, they prayed and worshiped. Then God did the incredible:

> Around midnight Paul and Silas were praying and singing hymns to God, and the other prisoners were listening. Suddenly, there was a massive earthquake, and the prison was shaken to its foundations. All the doors immediately flew open, and the chains of every prisoner fell off!
>
> — Acts 16:25–26, NLT

As Paul and Silas prayed and sang hymns to God, God inhabited their praise, and *everyone's* chains miraculously fell off! Not just their own. They testified to the Lord's power and love to other prisoners, leading to eternal salvation for both the jailer and his household. God also granted a boldness for Paul to speak up for his rights as a Roman citizen, and the officials had to come and openly apologize for their actions. This restored Paul and Silas' honor as they ministered in that community.

Praise creates a spiritual and unseen stronghold from which breaks forth in ambush and silences the believer's foes:

Through the praise of children and infants
You have established a stronghold against your enemies,
To silence the foe and the avenger.

— Psalm 8:2, NIV

That foe and avenger is Satan, trying to come against the people of God in numerous circumstances and through numerous people. But God silences him and causes him to cease, be still, and be ineffective. God will always lead you in triumph. You don't always have to know *how* He grants the victory, only that He will. The "how" is the mystery, adventure, and faith of the journey with Him.[10]

Our Pain and Victory

When one of our sons was in high school, he was bullied to the point that we did not know if he would survive without it affecting the rest of his life. We had a principal that was arrogant, and our son was gentle, kind and sensitive. This principal found it easier to deal with our son by putting the pressure on *him* to change rather than to deal with the bullies and the bully-type families in our community. We had absorbed all the consequences, including homeschooling and school transfers. They absorbed none.

Finally, I had enough. No one in our family could handle it anymore. I made the decision for victory; I didn't care what it cost me, and I no longer cared what it would cost my enemies. My son was broken.

I remember the day I declared the victory and attacked the situation in prayer, decreeing the greatness of God and the love of the Lord. I hit every injustice with an audacious and violent *ruwa* because I knew God was with me. I prayed through every level of the school division. I saw a picture in my mind's eye of a huge stone wall with enormous cracks forming. I asked God to expose every wicked and wrong thing in the school division and rearrange the staff. Not long

---

[10] The band *Rend* that has captured the power of the truth of God's love being our battle cry in music with lyrics that resonate with victory and the Holy Spirit in their song, "Every Giant Will Fall." Download it on iTunes and let it saturate your mind in truth and the joy of love's victory in your life.

after, the principal was removed from the school and the district rearranged those responsible for not helping my son, because of unrelated issues that God immediately exposed after prayer. A new fantastic principal was assigned to our community, and he supported our son and taught him how to assert himself.

God's love over my family was my banner and battle cry. No one could stand against God and me!

Another Victorious Ruwa

We were in a battle for the territory that God had assigned us to for the sake of souls. I was tired of some of the opposition and rejection we had been facing. If God had sent us, then it was time my situation lined up. I took a three-day absolute fast and blessed the situation and took a ferocious stand against every ungodly thing behind the rejection and opposition. I *ruwa'd* my victory that God had given me when He gave me the assignment. I stood firm against every closed door of man and *ruwa'd* some more. The walls fell flat and new favor opened to us. So much so, that the Lord laid it on the heart of one of history's most famous preachers and his wonderful staff to invite us to an all-expense paid ministry trip overseas to invest in our callings for souls. I felt like Jehoshaphat plundering the field when all his enemies lay still and lifeless on the ground. God can do mighty things when we settle it in our hearts that He is magnificent, powerful, victorious, deadly and lovingly praise Him as such. How great is our God!

Sacrifice of Praise

Praise needs to be the believer's go-to "method" not just to win the victory, but because He is worthy of it. As a good God, He deserves to be praised, and as a good Father He deserves to be thanked. In doing so, He tells His children what they can expect. David wrote that we should, "Enter his gates with thanksgiving; and into his courts with praise. Give thanks to him and praise his name" (Ps. 100:4 NIV). Believers can expect to be in His presence, which David said "is fullness of joy and at your right hand are pleasures forever more (Ps. 16:11 ESV). Now praise is no longer a sacrifice. His presence is full of joy.

Paul and Silas knew the sacrifice to praise in the jail. Jehoshaphat knew it on his way to fight a battle. King David knew it too—and often said things like "I will bless the Lord at all times" (Ps. 34:1 KJV), or "His praise will ever be on my lips" (Ps. 34:1). Through dark and painful challenges, David still magnified the Lord and His name over everything. Although praise and thanks bring victory, being steadfast and standing firm in faith also means praising God in times the follower of Jesus doesn't feel like it—simply because He is truly magnificent and completely deserving of our praise.

All Things Work Together for Good

When Paul told the Philippians to "rejoice always again I say rejoice" (Phil. 4:4), he spoke as one who had been through trials. Paul taught that the Lord is a Master Weaver and that He can take any situation in your life and work it together for good. He saw God turn a shipwreck into an opportunity to preach the gospel and a snakebite into an opportunity to heal. Paul saw God take a huge fight he had with one of his best friends, Barnabas, and turn it for good. Paul and Barnabas' division led to massive ministries, salvations, and miracles throughout the world. Paul trusted that God had a plan or could take something negative and make it outstanding.

You, too, can rejoice always. You can learn to rest more and more in the heat of challenges and battles, knowing they were in front of God first. He saw them a long way off, even before the foundation of the world. He has solutions to problems that haven't yet manifested and works His master-weaver skills for an incredible story. Consider Paul's words to the Ephesians and the Romans:

> He makes everything work according to His plan.
>
> — Ephesians 1:11, NLT

> And we know [with great confidence] that God [who is deeply concerned about us] causes all things to work together [as a plan]

> for good for those who love God, to those who are called according to His plan and purpose.
>
> — Romans 8:28, AMP

Both verses describe a knitting and a working through of details that seem to have deviated from the master plan. It affirms God can turn a person's mourning into dancing because He is not subject to circumstances. He is over them all. Because of this, Paul commissioned believers that in everything they should give thanks, "for this is the will of God in Christ Jesus for you (1 Thess. 5:18 KJV).

Thanking Him in advance is acknowledging how awesome He is and His infinitely great love. He will come through on your behalf or show you how to take hold of the victory. His character enables His children to give thanks regardless of what is seen. Paul wrote:

> Thanks be to God, who gives us the victory through our Lord Jesus Christ. Therefore, my beloved brethren, be steadfast, immovable, always abounding in the work of the Lord.
>
> — 1 Corinthians 15:57–58, NKJV

After thanks, Paul exhorts us to a call to be steadfast. This is the opposite of being tossed around like a wave on the sea. Remaining steadfast will allow you to abound in God's work, even when trials hit. Those trials will only prove Jesus as victor. He has overcome the world and has orchestrated your overcoming as well.

Joyce Meyer, a leading international teacher, grew up neglected and abused in so many ways. But God, in His goodness and compassion to her whole family, saw Joyce and moved her on a pathway to Himself. He loved her, taught her, healed her, and helped her. She did her part and worked hard to abound despite various trials and pain. Now, she ministers in that area of hurt to millions of hurting people around the world and teaches them to overcome through God. Her problems became her platform as she went through with God. She now thanks God those trials happened, because now she can serve, love, and help so many people.

You, too, can thank God before seeing any fruit because you can trust in His great love and character because He is working on your behalf.

Complain or Praise

There are two ways to respond to trials in life: to praise and thank God, or to murmur and complain. Complain in Hebrew is *laun* (*Strong's* H3885) and means, "to abide, remain and to stay permanent (in a bad sense)." In contrast, there is a pattern in Scripture where those who praise God are *raised out of* their challenges. When I realized that I had the power to decide to remain in my trial or be raised out of it, I asked God to test me in this area so I could learn and grow.

I didn't have to wait long for my first test. One day I saw a relative at a local event. I heard the Lord say, "Today is his day." I knew that the Lord wanted to save him. My relative and I chatted quite a bit, but then I lost track of him. I thought he had gone home so I hopped in the car, pulled out, and backed up onto a stump and found myself stuck. My axle and tire were pinned up on the stump. I opened the door, got out, and praised the Lord. I said, "God, I know you have an amazing plan in this. Work this out for something good." I had barely said amen when my relative came running out with a bunch of men to lift the vehicle off the stump. He hadn't left after all! When all four wheels were back on the ground, he asked me to his home for a visit and it was there he accepted the Lord Jesus Christ!

New Fries and New Believer

In another situation, I took my two sons out for a nice lunch. It was a three-hour drive into the city. On the way into the restaurant, I asked God to make me a blessing (and to bless us with a good meal).

As soon as our waitress arrived, I felt the love of God for her fill my heart. I then heard the Lord say, "She is in a crisis." I decided to see how the meal went and watch for an opening. Instead, I received another test.

She brought out two sides of cold fries. I had driven three hours for cold fries—six hours if you think about the return trip. I was curt with her. I felt the Holy Spirit bring correction to my heart, and I had to repent for my bad attitude. I began praising and thanking the Lord instead and hoped He would redeem my mistake. She came back with steaming fries; I looked at her and thanked her very much for doing that for us and told her how great they looked. I began to pour love on her the way she deserved. She gave me a big smile. We enjoyed the lunch and visited with her throughout the meal.

Soon it was time to go and I asked her if I could chat with her. She agreed and sat down beside me. I said, "As soon as I saw you, God spoke to my heart and said that you were in a crisis. Are you okay?" She began to cry and asked how I knew. I told her that her Father in heaven loved her and knew everything about her. She had received a call that morning that she needed surgery. She had cancer surgery two years prior and was terrified. We prayed and she gave her heart to Jesus Christ.

Try praising God and watch the atmosphere change. He loves it when His children celebrate His goodness before He acts, when they "Give thanks to the Lord, for He is good and His love endures forever" (Ps. 118:1 NLT).

Complaining is an Accusation

God hears the cries of His people, and He knows the difference between distress and complaining. Distress is not a problem for God. He is not angry or upset with you because of distress. In fact, it draws Him to you. Good fathers come to the aid of their children in distress. They also give promises, based on their love, to help and calm the child. And like a good dad does, God pictures a good future for His children. For example, God sent Moses to His people, Israel, to let them know He saw their distress and promised a better land (Ex. 3:7–8 NLT).

Problems arose, however, when they complained and murmured for lack of water. "'Give us water to drink!' they demanded. 'Are you trying to kill us, our children, and our livestock with thirst?'" (Ex. 17:2–3 NLT).

Don't miss the people's attitude: they demanded. I don't know about you, but when my kids demand something, it gets a little crazy at my house. I am a good parent. *Ask me.* Demanding means my kids don't believe I want to do something good for them and they think I am holding out on them.

Complaining, however, is not distress. Complaining is a negative declaration of character—an accusation. It is the exact opposite of praise. It declares someone or something is not living up to the other's standard. All the Israelites needed to do was ask God for help.

God had already delivered them from the distress of slavery. When the Israelite's grumbled in Exodus 17:2–3, they were complaining with accusation. Neither God nor Moses wanted to kill them. The lack of water was a challenge, but also an opportunity to see how God would provide. But they complained at each challenge and accused Moses and God of being potential murders and bringing them into difficulties just to kill them (see Ex. 16:3, 17:3, Num. 14:3). If God fills praise and inhabits it, what happens when people complain? And if a complaint is an accusation or a negative proclamation of someone's character, then what inhabits *that*?

Notice God's response to their complaints:

> Yes, I have heard the complaints the Israelites are making against me. Now tell them this: "As surely as I live, declares the Lord, I will do to you the very things I heard you say. You will all drop dead in this wilderness!"
>
> — Numbers 14:27–29, NLT

Sadly, God was to the Israelite's what they *allowed* Him to be and accused Him to be in their lives. They would have nothing else. Their complaining resulted in a period of wandering in the wilderness, and ultimately, in death.

Your Father is a good Father—a good God who has given up His only Son for you. As you face your challenges, battles, and trials, ask God for what you need with a thankful heart. Praise Him and watch Him set up spiritual ambushes and judge in your favor. Believe that He has your best in mind and can work all things together for good. Every trial that comes is an opportunity to see His greatness unfold. His love is your battle cry!

Reflect with the Holy Spirit

Welcome the Lord into a chatting time; learn while you sit at His feet. Use these questions to help open the conversation and ask God to give you answers to how to better praise and thank the Lord.

1. Lord, what in my life needs a *ruwa*, a victory shout? ______________
____
____

2. Who or what has raised its' fist against me and Your destiny? _______
____
____

3. Will You show me where am I complaining and remaining? Where am I praising and raising? ______________________________
____
____

4. How can I make Your love *my* battle cry? ______________________
____
____

5. How does my belief feel after I have praised, thanked, and *ruwa'd?* Do I notice anything different now? Do I notice anything over time with practice? ______________________________________
____
____

6. Can You trust me with some negativity? Can You trust me to believe Your good character when things go wrong? Do I believe You can work it together for good? ____________________________________
____
____

7. How do my battlefields look as I praise You? ____________________
____
____

CHAPTER 15 – REST AND COMMIT

Now we who have believed enter that rest, just as God has said, "So I declared on oath in my anger, 'They shall never enter my rest.'" And yet his works have been finished since the creation of the world. – Hebrews 4:3

I want you to imagine for a moment that your friend has a time machine. They have never lied to you and have been your faithful friend your entire life. One day, they came to you and said, "There is a race coming up and the prize is $10,000. I want you to practice for it because you are going to win. I know you are going to win!" The friend smiles at you confidently.

You give reasons why you can't win. You are ten pounds overweight. It might rain that day. You might need to buy runners, but you can't afford any new expenses. On and on you go and your friend keeps saying to do it. He even tells you that he knows things you do not and has seen you win at the finish line.

Your friend has never failed you. You can either keep worrying and reasoning or you can trust and go through the necessary motions from a place of rest and trust the guy.

Finished! Finished! Finished! You have been invited into something that God has finished. And yet his works have been finished since the creation of the world. (Heb 4:3)

There is a rest in knowing that God has not only authored your faith and destiny, He has finished it. He has seen you cross the finish line and only asks that you trust and commit. Don't worry about succeeding anymore. Just commit to moving forward from a place of rest. He has prepared everything you will ever need to fulfill His call on your life. If He has done it for me, a previously double-minded person, He will do it for you.

When you set yourself to obey His promptings, like Abraham, don't allow doubt to make you waver. Doubts will come, but get on the track, run your race with endurance and confidence, because you're going to win!

CONCLUSION

By now your new devoted heart has led you to a more steadfast and established life. You likely have cut off all the nattering heads and things have quietened down in your mind and soul. You are probably able to make your own decisions without polling people around you as often and are ready to do what God is prompting you to do. Others may still tell you the world doesn't need the dream God has placed in your heart, but remember: if God didn't need you and that dream, the dream would have left your heart by now.

You've learned to trust God's incredible character as your sure foundation and God's character will naturally lead to you trusting in Him and His righteous ways. A new confidence has begun to take root in your heart and soul; it was God's great pleasure to lay a firmer foundation in your life and to teach you how to stand and fight. He will continue to guide you in how to speak, how to stay silent, and how to praise.

Your times of reflection during this journey were times with the Lord where you examined your current situation and future endeavors. You, without knowing it, prepared your mind for action. When doubts come, you will know what pieces of the armor to use. When obstacles arise that appear to block your assignments, you will know to speak to them with the authority God gave you to establish the heavens and the earth. Never forget that He is good, and His love endures forever—and this love is what enables you to believe Him and stand firm. He has driven you into Himself and made you like a nail in a sure place.

So, go ahead! Make decisions, take those new steps, speak the promises He has whispered to your heart, and live. May He hang on you the glory of His house, that the world may know and see His excellence in your future work and endeavors.

And I will fasten him as a nail in a sure place; and he shall be for a glorious throne to his father's house. — Isaiah 22:23, KJV

Reflect with the Holy Spirit

Invite the Lord to reflect with you over your journey into becoming a steadfast and courageous child of God. Enjoy this time with God quietly and with unrushed peace. Relish in the fact that He is present.

1. What was one of my greatest moments of clarity? How did I feel prompted to respond? ______________________________

____

____

2. What was one of Your favorite moments, Lord, as You watched me learn and process? ______________________________

____

____

3. How am I feeling now? Are there any new ideas about how I want to live differently? ______________________________

____

____

4. How do I feel about my God assignments now? Is it time to embrace a new one? Am I excited? ______________________________

____

____

5. What am I celebrating at the end of this journey? What are You celebrating? Help me to savor this joy, not rush out of it, and enjoy Your presence. ____
____
____

Thank the Lord and praise Him for a little while. Take your time. Don't force it; relax and rest with a thankful and joyful heart. Tell Him why you love Him and that you're glad He was with you on this journey.

Fini!

AUTHOR'S TESTIMONY

I remember the first time I overheard a person say that I was flighty. I was just a child at the time, but I trusted that person completely so therefore their assessment of me must be true. I'm confident the comment wasn't meant to grip my life and was only said in passing. I believed their testimony more than I believed anything else. The result was that I no longer trusted myself to make decisions or to be competent and powerful. It was the beginning of the double-mindedness that held my life in its grip for decades. The doubt in myself caused me to be unable to give myself wholly to a decision or even to God, for what could be trusted? How could I, this flighty and flawed person, even be devoted and loyal to any decision or God if I was not steadfast and solid? Every decision was a flip-flopping ordeal as part of my heart was loyal to God and part to my fears, insecurities or worries.

As God taught me more about His steadfast character, I decided it was time to see what would happen if I repented of all the things that pulled me away from trusting Him. I began to build my life on the stability of God's character and ways. He helped me get over the fear of man. I had to learn to break free from the ideals that people held and walk in the word of God and the promptings of the Holy Spirit. Only Jesus' opinion began to matter. My life began to take on fresh boldness and courage with each step I took in lining up my life with what the Holy Spirit was saying. He provided all the finances to do His work with a Heavenly abundance. I felt the smile of my Father get wider and wider with every "yes".

He began to touch on other areas like faith and forgiveness. He taught me that I could not receive His faithful and loving forgiveness, then be unfaithful in giving it away to others. My heart had to be undivided in this area and whole because my faith in Him and His promises worked through love. My faith and fresh courage would work best when I walked in harmony with Him.

Bit by bit, peace began to fill my soul and life. Miraculously, I went from being double-minded to single-minded in about 2 ½ years. I barely recognize myself or my life. With an undivided heart, He established my life and ended my double-mindedness. Flip flopping on decisions became a thing of the past and confidence replaced confusion.

I was fruitless in my endeavors for decades but at the culmination of this book, and processing these beautiful lessons with the Lord, I have opened my own online anti-trafficking missions school, written a book, preached and seen people saved, healed and delivered. I have hosted my first powerful event which gathered people from over 20 communities as they pursued God for revival. I have also done almost $80,000 in ministry work as well as the admin to support that work in 9 months. I have been to Africa with one of God's most influential evangelists, Daniel Kolenda and encouraged new preachers by sharing my pulpits. In all these things, I have had to fight cowardice, the fear of man, doubt, the idols of money, status and other things. I have learned to believe with a fidelity, obedience, and sell myself out for God. I have learned to go to the maypoles even if it's all by myself. I've learned to keep my words in check and suit up to fight the battles of doubt and unbelief. I have learned, above all else, that His love and character is the foundation of my peace and stability and will never be taken from me.

As I committed myself to Jesus, I discovered that He trusted me with assignments for my life and for the world and that He was even more committed to me than I was to Him. God mentored and discipled me out of other loyalties, loves and the fears that were holding me back from Him and from being my best me for the world. He championed me through by His power and His Holy Spirit to bring me to the place where I can champion others. I've gone from double-minded to single-minded and from flighty to fearless and free.

These have been the best few years of my life and the whole world is at my feet ready for me to take even more radical steps of faith and obedience. With Jesus in my heart and His character as my firm foundation, I will have the steadfastness of His faithfulness beneath the soles of my feet as solid ground beneath each step. The world He died to save awaits my next "yes". The world Jesus died to save also awaits your next "yes". So, enter His rest and the finished works He has ordained for you.

APPENDIX A – HOW TO HEAR GOD'S VOICE

By Dr. Mark Virkler

She had done it again! Instead of coming straight home from school like she was supposed to, she had gone to her friend's house. Without permission. Without our knowledge. Without doing her chores.

With a ministering household that included remnants of three struggling families plus our own toddler and newborn, my wife simply couldn't handle all the work on her own. Everyone had to pull their own weight. Everyone had age-appropriate tasks they were expected to complete. At fourteen, Rachel and her younger brother were living with us while her parents tried to overcome lifestyle patterns that had resulted in the children running away to escape the dysfunction. I felt sorry for Rachel, but, honestly my wife was my greatest concern.

Now Rachel had ditched her chores to spend time with her friends. It wasn't the first time, but if I had anything to say about it, it would be the last. I intended to lay down the law when she got home and make it very clear that if she was going to live under my roof, she would obey my rules.

But…she wasn't home yet. And I had recently been learning to hear God's voice more clearly. Maybe I should try to see if I could hear anything from Him about the situation. Maybe He could give me a way to get her to do what she was supposed to (i.e. what I wanted her to do). So I went to my office and reviewed what the Lord had been teaching me from Habakkuk 2:1,2: "I will stand on my guard post and station myself on the rampart; And I will keep watch to see what He will speak to me…Then the Lord answered me and said, 'Record the vision….'"

Habakkuk said, "I will stand on my guard post..." (Hab. 2:1). **The first key to hearing God's voice is to go to a quiet place and still our own thoughts and emotions.** Psalm 46:10 encourages us to be still, let go, cease striving, and know that He is God. In Psalm 37:7 we are called to "be still before the Lord and wait patiently for Him." There is a deep inner knowing in our spirits that each of us can experience when we quiet our flesh and our minds. Practicing the art of biblical meditation helps silence the outer noise and distractions clamoring for our attention.

I didn't have a guard post but I did have an office, so I went there to quiet my temper and my mind. Loving God through a quiet worship song is one very effective way to become still. In 2 Kings 3, Elisha needed a word from the Lord so he said, "Bring me a minstrel," and as the minstrel played, the Lord spoke. I have found that playing a worship song on my autoharp is the quickest way for me to come to stillness. I need to choose my song carefully; boisterous songs of praise do not bring me to stillness, but rather gentle songs that express my love and worship. And it isn't enough just to sing the song into the cosmos – I come into the Lord's presence most quickly and easily when I use my godly imagination to see the truth that He is right here with me and I sing my songs to Him, personally.

"I will keep watch to see," said the prophet. To receive the pure word of God, it is very important that my heart be properly focused as I become still, because my focus is the source of the intuitive flow. If I fix my eyes upon Jesus (Heb. 12:2), the intuitive flow comes from Jesus. But if I fix my gaze upon some desire of my heart, the intuitive flow comes out of that desire. To have a pure flow I must become still and carefully fix my eyes upon Jesus. Quietly worshiping the King and receiving out of the stillness that follows quite easily accomplishes this.

So I used **the second key to hearing God's voice: As you pray, fix the eyes of your heart upon Jesus, seeing in the Spirit the dreams and visions of Almighty God.** Habakkuk was actually looking for vision as he prayed. He opened the eyes of his heart, and looked into the spirit world to see what God wanted to show him.

God has always spoken through dreams and visions, and He specifically said that they would come to those upon whom the Holy Spirit is poured out (Acts 2:1-4, 17).

Being a logical, rational person, observable facts that could be verified by my physical senses were the foundations of my life, including my spiritual life. I had never thought of opening the eyes of my heart and looking for vision. However, I have come to believe that this is exactly what God wants me to do. He gave me eyes in my heart to see in the spirit the vision and movement of Almighty God. There is an active spirit world all around us, full of angels, demons, the Holy Spirit, the omnipresent Father, and His omnipresent Son, Jesus. The only reasons for me not to see this reality are unbelief or lack of knowledge.

In his sermon in Acts 2:25, Peter refers to King David's statement: "I saw the Lord always in my presence; for He is at my right hand, so that I will not be shaken." The original psalm makes it clear that this was a decision of David's, not a constant supernatural visitation: "I have set (literally, I have placed) the Lord continually before me; because He is at my right hand, I will not be shaken" (Ps.16:8). Because David knew that the Lord was always with him, he determined in his spirit to *see* that truth with the eyes of his heart as he went through life, knowing that this would keep his faith strong.

In order to see, we must look. Daniel saw a vision in his mind and said, "I was looking...I kept looking...I kept looking" (Dan. 7:2, 9, 13). As I pray, I look for Jesus, and I watch as He speaks to me, doing and saying the things that are on His heart. Many Christians will find that if they will only look, they will see. Jesus is Emmanuel, God with us (Matt. 1:23). It is as simple as that. You can see Christ present with you because Christ ***is*** present with you. In fact, the vision may come so easily that you will be tempted to reject it, thinking that it is just you. But if you persist in recording these visions, your doubt will soon be overcome by faith as you recognize that the content of them could only be birthed in Almighty God.

Jesus demonstrated the ability of living out of constant contact with God, declaring that He did nothing on His own initiative, but only what He saw the Father doing, and heard the Father saying (Jn. 5:19,20,30). What an incredible way to live!

Is it possible for us to live out of divine initiative as Jesus did? Yes! We must simply fix our eyes upon Jesus. The veil has been torn, giving access into the immediate presence of God, and He calls us to draw near (Lk. 23:45; Heb. 10:19-22). "I pray that the eyes of your heart will be enlightened...."

When I had quieted my heart enough that I was able to picture Jesus without the distractions of my own ideas and plans, I was able to "keep watch to see what He will speak to me." I wrote down my question: "Lord, what should I do about Rachel?"

Immediately the thought came to me, "She is insecure." Well, that certainly wasn't my thought! Her behavior looked like rebellion to me, not insecurity.

But like Habakkuk, I was coming to know the sound of God speaking to me (Hab. 2:2). Elijah described it as a still, small voice (I Kings 19:12). I had previously listened for an inner audible voice, and God does speak that way at times. However, I have found that usually, God's voice comes as spontaneous thoughts, visions, feelings, or impressions.

For example, haven't you been driving down the road and had a thought come to you to pray for a certain person? Didn't you believe it was God telling you to pray? What did God's voice sound like? Was it an audible voice, or was it a spontaneous thought that lit upon your mind?

Experience indicates that we perceive spirit-level communication as spontaneous thoughts, impressions and visions, and Scripture confirms this in many ways. For example, one definition of *paga*, a Hebrew word for intercession, is "a chance encounter or an accidental intersecting." When God lays people on our hearts, He does it through *paga*, a chance-encounter thought "accidentally" intersecting our minds.

So **the third key to hearing God's voice is recognizing that God's voice in your heart often sounds like a flow of spontaneous thoughts.** Therefore, when I want to hear from God, I tune to chance-encounter or spontaneous thoughts.

Finally, God told Habakkuk to record the vision (Hab. 2:2). This was not an isolated command. The Scriptures record many examples of individual's prayers and God's replies, such as the Psalms, many of the prophets, and Revelation. I have found that obeying this final principle amplified my confidence in my ability to hear God's voice so that I could finally make living out of His initiatives a way of life. The **fourth key, two-way journaling or the writing out of your prayers and God's answers, brings great freedom in hearing God's voice.**

I have found two-way journaling to be a fabulous catalyst for clearly discerning God's inner, spontaneous flow, because as I journal I am able to write in faith for long periods of time, simply believing it is God. I know that what I believe I have received from God must be tested. However, testing involves doubt and doubt blocks divine communication, so I do not want to test while I am trying to receive. (See James 1:5-8.) With journaling, I can receive in faith, knowing that when the flow has ended I can test and examine it carefully.

So I wrote down what I believed He had said: "She is insecure."

But the Lord wasn't done. I continued to write the spontaneous thoughts that came to me: "Love her unconditionally. She is flesh of your flesh and bone of your bone."

My mind immediately objected: She is not flesh of my flesh. She is not related to me at all – she is a foster child, just living in my home temporarily. It was definitely time to test this "word from the Lord"!

There are three possible sources of thoughts in our minds: ourselves, satan and the Holy Spirit. It was obvious that the words in my journal did not come from my own mind – I certainly didn't see her as insecure *or* flesh of my flesh. And I sincerely doubted that satan would encourage me to love anyone unconditionally!

Okay, it was starting to look like I might have actually received counsel from the Lord. It was consistent with the names and character of God as revealed in the Scripture, and totally contrary to the names and character of the enemy. So that meant that I was hearing from the Lord, and He wanted me to see the situation in a different light. Rachel was my daughter – part of my family not by blood but by the hand of God Himself. The chaos of her birth home had created deep insecurity about her worthiness to be loved by anyone, including me and including God. Only the unconditional love of the Lord expressed through an imperfect human would reach her heart.

But there was still one more test I needed to perform before I would have absolute confidence that this was truly God's word to me: I needed confirmation from someone else whose spiritual discernment I trusted. So I went to my wife and shared what I had received. I knew if I could get her validation, especially since she was the one most wronged in the situation, then I could say, at least to myself, "Thus sayeth the Lord."

Needless to say, Patti immediately and without question confirmed that the Lord had spoken to me. My entire planned lecture was forgotten. I returned to my office anxious to hear more. As the Lord planted a new, supernatural love for Rachel within me, He showed me what to say and how to say it to not only address the current issue of household responsibility, but the deeper issues of love and acceptance and worthiness.

Rachel and her brother remained as part of our family for another two years, giving us many opportunities to demonstrate and teach about the Father's love, planting spiritual seeds in thirsty soil. We weren't perfect and we didn't solve all of her issues, but because I had learned to listen to the Lord, we were able to avoid creating more brokenness and separation.

The four simple keys that the Lord showed me from Habakkuk have been used by people of all ages, from four to a hundred and four, from every continent, culture and denomination, to break through into intimate two-way conversations with their loving Father and dearest Friend. Omitting any one of the keys will prevent you from receiving all He wants to say to you. The order of the keys is not important, just that you *use them all*. Embracing all four, by faith, can change your life. Simply quiet yourself down, tune to spontaneity, look for vision, and journal. He is waiting to meet you there.

You will be amazed when you journal! Doubt may hinder you at first, bı throw it off, reminding yourself that it is a biblical concept, and that God is present, speaking to His children. Relax. When we cease our labors and enter His rest, God is free to flow (Heb. 4:10).

Why not try it for yourself, right now? Sit back comfortably, take out your pen and paper, and smile. Turn your attention toward the Lord in praise and worship, seeking His face. Many people have found the music and visionary prayer called "A Stroll Along the Sea of Galilee" helpful in getting them started. You can listen to it and download it free at www.CWGMinistries.org/Galilee.

After you write your question to Him, become still, fixing your gaze on Jesus. You will suddenly have a very good thought. Don't doubt it; simply write it down. Later, as you read your journaling, you, too, will be blessed to discover that you are indeed dialoguing with God. If you wonder if it is really the Lord speaking to you, share it with your spouse or a friend. Their input will encourage your faith and strengthen your commitment to spend time getting to know the Lover of your soul more intimately than you ever dreamed possible.

Is It *Really* God?

Five ways to be sure what you're hearing is from Him:

1) Test the Origin (1 Jn. 4:1)

Thoughts from our own minds are progressive, with one thought leading to the next, however tangentially. Thoughts from the spirit world are spontaneous. The Hebrew word for true prophecy is *naba,* which literally means to bubble up, whereas false prophecy is *ziyd* meaning to boil up. True words from the Lord will bubble up from our innermost being; we don't need to cook them up ourselves.

2) Compare It to Biblical Principles

God will never say something to you personally which is contrary to His universal revelation as expressed in the Scriptures. If the Bible clearly states that g is a sin, no amount of journaling can make it right. Much of what ..urnal about will not be specifically addressed in the Bible, however, so ..nderstanding of biblical principles is also needed.

3) Compare It to the Names and Character of God as Revealed in the Bible

Anything God says to you will be in harmony with His essential nature. Journaling will help you get to *know* God personally, but knowing what the Bible says *about* Him will help you discern what words are from Him. Make sure the tenor of your journaling lines up with the character of God as described in the names of the Father, Son and Holy Spirit.

4) Test the Fruit (Matt. 7:15-20)

What effect does what you are hearing have on your soul and your spirit? Words from the Lord will quicken your faith and increase your love, peace and joy. They will stimulate a sense of humility within you as you become more aware of Who God is and who you are. On the other hand, any words you receive which cause you to fear or doubt, which bring you into confusion or anxiety, or which stroke your ego (especially if you hear something that is "just for you alone – no one else is worthy") must be immediately rebuked and rejected as lies of the enemy.

5) Share It with Your Spiritual Counselors (Prov. 11:14)

We are members of a Body! A cord of three strands is not easily broken and God's intention has always been for us to grow together. Nothing will increase your faith in your ability to hear from God like having it confirmed by two or three other people! Share it with your spouse, your parents, your friends, your elder, your group leader, even your grown children can be your sounding board. They don't need to be perfect or super-spiritual; they just need to love you, be committed to being available to you, have a solid biblical orientation, and most importantly, they must also willingly and easily receive counsel. Avoid the authoritarian who insists that because of their standing in the church or with God, they no longer need to listen to others. Find two or three people and let them confirm that you are hearing from God!

The book *4 Keys to Hearing God's Voice* is available at www.CWGMinistries.org

Made in the USA
Monee, IL
10 February 2020

21588268R00128